ROYAL CULINARY

COLLECTIONS™

Royal Caribbean
International
C O O K B O O K

Royal Caribbean
International
C O O K B O O K

R U D I   S O D A M I N

RIZZOLI
NEW YORK

First published in the United States of America in 2001 by
RIZZOLI INTERNATIONAL PUBLICATIONS, INC.
300 Park Avenue South
New York, NY 10010

ISBN: 0-8478-2382-2

Food Photography by Herb Schmitz
Product photography by Taddler Photography
Design by Lynne Yeamans

Distributed by St. Martin's Press

Printed and bound in Singapore

This book is dedicated to all of the men and women who make up our Culinary Service Team in gratitude for their tireless efforts in making great dining experiences onboard our beautiful ships.

acknowledgments

Without the following people, this book would never be what it is today. I would like to thank these people for their support: Richard Fain, Jack Williams, Adam Goldstein, Michael Bayley, Daniel Hanrahan, Richard Henley, Max Horbiger, Patrick Irons, Lynn Martenstein, Tom Murrill, Doug Santoni, Barbara Shrut, Noelle Sipos; Michele Smith, David Stanley, and Nancy Wheatley; all of my Senior and Executive Chefs for their hard work and dedication: Josef Jungwirth, Fritz Halbedl, Albert Kopp, Paul Mooney, Wolfgang Saurer, Romeo Bueno, Burghardt Schnabel, Andreas Tuma, Thomas Barth, Guenther Bartschte, Michael Edletzberger, Helga Finnsdottir, Martin Grabenhofer, Nestor Guevara, Alfred Hauser, Vallet Knight, Sanjay Kumar, Herbert Ludwig, Thomas Pelloschek, Markland Priestley, Christina Ross, Raymond Southern, Spencer Tomlinson; our sous-chefs: Sanjay Argawal, Danilo Austero, Rana Bir, Samuel Boyd, Nelson Cabral, Don Croitor, Hugh Cunningham, Nethaji Dasarathan, Mark Delmas, Nelson Gonzalez, Hamilton Hewitt, Trevor Kramp, Anil Kumar, John Mascarenhas, Raja Ravi Saunder, Claude Rouat, Martin Scott, Seidy Solderholm, Frederick Taylor, Huber Werner, Arthur Williams, Allan Winder, and Sandra Wolf; all of our hotel directors: David Armitage, Carlos Bouzon, Tony Curtis, Fred DeCosse, Tony Fitzsimmons, Bernhard Friesacher, Raimund Gschaider, Laila Hassan, Shakir Hussein, Ken Jacques, Bjorn Julseth, Sigi Konetzny, Helmut Leikauf, Tony Muresu, Patrick Olin, Tony O'Prey, Sue Richardson, Martin Rissley, David Stephenson, Hermann Stingeder, Robert Taggart, Bob Tavadia, Amanda White; our F&B Managers and Maitre'd's; my home office culinary team: Mitchell Berman, Deborah Blankenship, Lisa Delgado, Randi Galex, Dee Gretzler, Corinne Lewis, and Karen Woolley; the dedicated Rizzoli team including Marta Hallett, Ima Ebong, Lynne Yeamans and Kristen Schilo; the entire Royal Caribbean International family; Julie Mautner; Herb Schmitz; Pat Doyle; and last, but certainly not least, Monika Velgos. I especially want to thank Maria Sastre, for without her vision and perseverance, this book would not be in your hands today.

table of contents

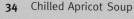

f o r e w o r d

What's cooking in your kitchen? I guess you are!

Cooking can be a celebration of all the senses: from the aromas and textures of fresh ingredients, to the beauty of a table set for family or friends, to the way that a good meal stirs your taste buds as well as your mood and memories.

Cooking is also a celebration of nature, of the cycles of seasonality, of our relationship to the earth and to the sustaining bounty of the harvest.

Cooking is a fascinating part of our cultural heritage. What we eat and drink—and why and when— speaks volumes about where we came from and who we are. This is why I love it and why I do it for a living. This is why I do it at home as often as I can.

From the frequency with which new cookbooks and food magazines cross my desk (not to mention everything food-related that's flitting across my computer and television screen these days), I'm clearly not alone.

When I cook for my family and friends, they can see how much they mean to me. By nourishing their bodies, I hope to feed their souls as well. But when you're a person who loves to cook for others, it doesn't matter if it's your family at the table or 3,000 hungry passengers. The pleasure and the passion are the same.

At Royal Caribbean, we have a culinary team of thousands, representing every nationality possible, working together to provide our guests with delicious and comforting food, prepared perfectly from the freshest ingredients, presented impeccably and served in a gracious, yet relaxed, setting.

At home, of course, it's just you in the kitchen, with perhaps a helper or two if you're lucky. But all you really need is a sense of adventure, some humor and this book. I hope you'll use these recipes as guidelines, and sprinkle them liberally with your imagination. Cooking is a science, but it's an art and a craft as well. And that's where the fun comes in. Be sure to do some advance preparation if you are entertaining, to maximize the time you spend with your family and friends.

To quote James Beard, who is considered by many to be the father of modern American cuisine: "I don't like gourmet cooking or this cooking or that cooking. I like good cooking." It is in that spirit that I selected these recipes for this cookbook, from our ships. Each one has been adapted for home kitchens. You will find wonderful, easy-to-prepare dishes, made from ingredients that are readily available and popular with families the world over, that are sure to work each and every time.

I hope that you love this book. It couldn't have been done without the support from Royal Caribbean International, and from Jack Williams, Adam Goldstein, Josef Jungwirth and especially Maria Sastre. Thank you for letting me share our cuisine with you.

Bon Appetit!
Rudi Sodamin

i n t r o d u c t i o n

Throughout the rich history of Royal Caribbean International, we have had a long-standing tradition to provide our guests with culinary pleasures from across the globe. Some of the fondest cruise memories center on the taste sensations carefully prepared and served by our international crew.

We hope that our *Royal Caribbean International Cookbook* will allow you to create our magical tastes in your own kitchen. The recipes that follow have delighted guests from more than 120 different countries and reflect the heritage of our multinational culinary staff.

The range of cuisines we have drawn upon from around the world will enchant you and yours in the comfort of your home. We invite you to join us as we journey through a world of tastes that only the unparalleled talents of Royal Caribbean International chefs could create.

Jack L. Williams
President, Royal Caribbean International

a word about ingredients

OLIVE OIL Always use extra-virgin olive oil. Never buy 100% pure olive oil, which is much less delicate and hardly has any olive flavor. A good extra-virgin olive oil usually has a deep green color. (However, the color is not always an indication of the quality, since many producers press the leaves along with the olives to extract chlorophyll, which creates the deep green color.) Next, look for a rich texture and a strong and very aromatic olive flavor. You will have to taste-test by comparing the flavors among a few small bottles. I have developed several blends of infused olive oils under the Royal Caribbean Culinary Collections™ brand. One oil in particular is olive oil infused with rosemary and garlic.

VINEGAR When I want to add a soft, delicate flavor, I use a good red and a good white wine vinegar. (But don't confuse white wine vinegar with white vinegar—the white vinegar is wonderful for cleaning your floors and windows, but please, never use it in your food!) Rice wine vinegar is usually very mild, and it is perfect for when you need just a slight hint of vinegar flavor. Apple cider vinegar adds the beautiful and delicate fragrance of apple to any sauce. My favorite, which I use in so many of my recipes, is balsamic vinegar. This aromatic vinegar is aged for at least four years in oak, chestnut, ash or cherry barrels, and can be aged for 50 years or more. Usually the longer it ages, the sweeter it becomes. For cooking, however, use the balsamic vinegars you find in the supermarket. They should be brilliant and clear, but never cloudy. A good balsamic vinegar should have a sharp, pungent aftertaste. I recommend using infused balsamic vinegar. Some of my creations include cherry pepper infused sherry vinegar, fig balsamic and raspberry balsamic vinegar. The latter of the two are really great to use on salad.

HERBS I have this "thing" about dried herbs found in bottles at the supermarket. Every jar I open smells the same to me. So, except when you are making dried bread crumbs, try to always use fresh herbs. I always thought there could be something better than those typical store bought herbs, therefore I have developed my own spice blends for each category—beef, poultry, fish, veal, lamb, vegetables, etc. This will definitely make life easier. However, if you have access to fresh herbs, I suggest using them.

GARLIC Try to choose heads of garlic with tight, papery skin and firm cloves. I never use a garlic press, since I find it easier to smash the garlic between a cutting board and the flat side of my chef's knife. The papery skin will slip right off and all you need to do is chop it. Please do not overcook, as it may become bitter.

PHYLLO PASTRY I have used frozen phyllo (or filo) pastry in several recipes, even though it can be somewhat difficult to work with at times. Critical steps for success are letting it defrost at room temperature for at least six hours before you use it and working with it very slowly and carefully. It's a great dough to use because it's low in fat, and I love the end result—a crispy, light, and very flavorful pastry.

PARMIGIANO-REGGIANO There are certain ingredients that are not replaceable in my kitchen, and whenever I call for Parmesan cheese in any recipe, I mean Parmigiano-Reggiano. The taste and consistency of this cheese is matchless. Any Italian market worthy of its name will surely have Parmigiano-Reggiano cheese.

TOMATOES A truly ripe tomato is certainly hard to find in any market. But when you do find it—it is incredible! I love a vine-ripened tomato that actually smells and tastes like a tomato. When buying tomatoes, select the ripest ones, making sure they aren't too soft. Never refrigerate them, as it will interfere with their flavor and texture. And, when you cook tomatoes, be sure to peel and seed them, unless the skin and seeds will be strained away later.

basic equipment

IMMERSION BLENDER   A must for every kitchen, this tall, narrow blender has a very sharp blade at the end. It can be inserted directly into a saucepan, transforming an ordinary vegetable soup into a wonderfully creamy dish. You can save a sauce that has "separated" by emulsifying it with this blender. It's also very useful for eliminating lumps.

FOOD PROCESSOR   This marvelous kitchen appliance chops, dices, grinds, and purées almost any food. I cannot imagine cooking without it! You really need only one medium-size processor, but you may want to get a mini-processor as well. These are great for chopping a couple of shallots or garlic cloves, or a few sprigs of fresh herbs. A coffee grinder is also wonderful for pulverizing things like cinnamon sticks, nutmeg, or tapioca pearls.

TONGS   It's amazing how much I depend on my tongs; I would be totally lost without them. They are like an extension of my fingers. If you are a beginner, get spring-loaded stainless-steel tongs, no longer than 12 inches (30 cm).

WHISKS   You need only two basic styles: a "sauce whisk" for blending sauce and soup ingredients, and a "balloon whisk" with pear-shaped thin wires, which allow you to incorporate air into cream or eggs for maximum fluffiness. Heavy-duty stainless-steel whisks work best.

SIEVES   You should have two kinds of sieves; one with a fine mesh and one with a medium mesh. The coarse netting is useful for straining stock, while the finer weave helps to create a silky texture when finishing a sauce. Again, I recommend that you buy the finest quality stainless-steel sieves you can afford—they will last you a lifetime.

POTS AND PANS   At my cooking demonstrations, people always want to know: Which brands of pots do I use and what are my feelings about nonstick? I love to use stainless-steel pots, as they are nonreactive to most food. And although I disliked nonstick pans at one time, I now swear by them. You should have one small and one medium sauté pan, a couple of medium-size saucepans, and a large—about 14-quart (14 liters)—stockpot. A small rondeau—6-inch deep (15 cm) Dutch oven—is also fantastic for risotto and pasta dishes.

CHEESE GRATER   Freshly grated Parmesan cheese makes a world of difference when preparing any pasta dish that calls for the ingredient. After you use freshly grated Parmigiano-Reggiano on top of a steaming risotto, you will never return to those prepared products found in a supermarket.

ZESTER   Usually made of stainless steel, this gadget has four or five tiny cutting holes that remove the outer skin of citrus without the white section, which is somewhat bitter. This tool is not exactly a must, but you will find it fun to use and very efficient.

TABLETOP MIXER   This may be one of the most expensive small appliances you'll buy; prices range from $150 to $350. But if you plan on baking wonderful cheesecakes or chiffon cakes, you will find it very useful. Buy yourself a very sturdy model, preferably one that comes with two bowls of at least $4^{1}/_{2}$ quarts (4.25 liters), a whip, a paddle, and a dough hook.

SPATULA   Essential for cleaning all ingredients out of mixing bowls. The heat-resistant ones are especially useful. You can use them as you sauté fish, cook pancakes, and of course, scrape your mixing bowls.

KNIVES   A knife may be the most important and often-used tool in your kitchen. Buy a high-quality knife and, if you take care of it, it will last you a lifetime. An inexpensive one will become dull, lose its balance, and will only last a couple of years. A good knife will feel very comfortable and balanced in your hand. I recommend that you buy a high-carbon stainless-steel blade with a full tang (that is, the blade continues into the knife handle) that is as long as the entire handle. Your starter kit should include:

• A paring knife, with a 3-inch (7.5 cm) blade for peeling fruit and vegetables.

• A boning knife, whose rigid 6-to-7-inch (15-17.5 cm) blade fits between the meat and bone or skin, making it easy to debone poultry or meat.

• An 8-to-10-inch (20-25cm) chef's knife, for chopping, slicing and dicing. Buy the best you can afford.

• A slicer, a very thin knife with a 10-inch (25 cm) blade—a must for slicing cooked meat, poultry and cured salmon without tearing the meat.

• A steel, which does not sharpen knives, but will keep them sharp if used regularly. If your knives become dull, you'll need a sharpening stone (or professional sharpening which can be done by a knife store).

Pastry Bags   A pastry bag can transform many preparations into masterpieces, easily and inexpensively. The best part is you don't need to be an expert. You just need a 14-to-18-inch (35-45 cm) bag, plus two plain tips—$1/4$ and $1/2$ inch— (6.3 mm and 1.25 cm) and a few decorative tips.

basic knife techniques

Basic knife skills are not only necessary for the pleasure and aesthetics of your cooking experience, but they are also important for your safety. Practicing accuracy and safety will eventually turn into speed, but what's the hurry? It is an old chef's adage, but it is true that a dull knife will cut you worse than a sharp one. Therefore, it is extremely important to keep a good edge on all of your knives.

First, some helpful hints: Your chef's knife, also known as a French knife, is most useful and recommended for the different cuts used in cooking. Its rounded blade edge is what makes it unique. Take advantage of the rounded blade to rock it back and forth (like a rocking chair). A potato is good for knife practice. Wash it well and peel it. You will want to cut it into some manageable lengths, $1^{1}/2$ to 2 inches (3.75-5 cm) long. One thing to keep in mind: have the nails of your free hand firmly on the potato. This will form your

knuckles into a flat surface, safe from the knife. You always want that hand to look like a claw when slicing and dicing.

Let's get started!   Take one of the potato segments and give it four sides, so if you hold it up and look at the end, you see a square.

We'll begin the julienne cut:

1. Hold the potato with your fingers on the top of the squared-off potato and looking at the top, cut a "sheet" $1/8$ inch (3.1 mm) thick off the side.

2. Continue this until you have come as close as possible to your fingers. Stack the "sheets" up, maybe only three or four high.

3. Cut the sheets into $1/8$-inch (3.1 mm) sticks.

1. Lay your julienne cuts evenly into a pile.

2. Measure $1/8$ inch (3.1 mm) from the end.

3. Rock your chef's knife gently but straight to cut them into cubes. That's all there is to it!

In most recipes, you will find the terms used most often are chopped, diced and minced, when referring to knife cuts. To chop is to roughly cut pieces into the same size. Dice refers to consistent cubes of food of whatever size is called for in the recipe. Mince is to chop very finely. Good examples are minced garlic or ginger. Here is a case when rocking your chef's knife is quite handy. The palm of your free hand rests lightly on the bottom third of the knife while you rock it back and forth over the food.

The bâtonnet and macedoine cuts are done exactly the same way as the julienne and brunoise, respectively, except that the bâtonnet is $1/4$ inch (6.3 mm) instead of $1/8$ inch (3.1 mm). And macedoine is a $1/4$ inch (6.3 mm)cube. They are exactly two times the size of the julienne and brunoise.

OTHER POPULAR VEGETABLE CUTS INCLUDE THE FOLLOWING:

Chiffonade is a cut most often applied to cabbage or lettuce leaves, leeks or large-leaf herbs. The easiest way to cut in chiffonade is to roll the lettuce or herb leaf into a tight cigar shape and, with a very sharp knife, make very thin crosswise slices. The result is thin shreds of vegetable or herb, much thinner than julienne.

As you read recipes, particularly professional ones, you may note other knife cuts that carry French or just plain confusing names. One such is concassé, pronounced "conk-uh-say," which usually refers to peeled, seeded and chopped tomatoes. The same technique may be used to peel and pit apricots or peaches, as well. It is usually done when presentation is a key element.

Here is how it's done.

1. Put on a pot of water, enough to immerse a tomato, and bring it to a boil.

2. Fill a bowl with ice and water, again, enough to immerse a tomato.

3. With the tip of your paring knife, make an X on the bottom of the tomato (opposite from the stem end), just cutting through the outer skin, not the meat.

4. Then, by angling your paring knife, remove the core only. What's key here is to remove only the core, no more, no less.

5. When the water is boiling, drop the tomato in. After approximately 30 seconds, or when the skin at the X begins to peel back, remove the tomato and plunge it into the ice water. Now you have a blanched tomato!

6. When it's cooled down, and not water logged, take it out and pat it dry. Slide off the skin and discard.

7. Cut the tomato either top to bottom or through the middle. Gently squeeze the seeds out and discard them. Some chefs will cut the tomato into fourths, then pull the seeds out. Then, roughly dice the tomato.

appetizers

THEY MAY BE CALLED BY A VARIETY OF NAMES— *hors d' oeuvres,* starters, finger foods, small portions, first courses, *mezze*—but everyone knows an appetizer when they see one. Virtually every culture has some form of them (more likely, hundreds of them) in its cuisine. In China, appetizers are known as *dim sum* (literally, "heart warmers"). In France, they're sometimes called *amuse bouche* or *amuse-gueule*, both of which translate loosely as "delight the palate." It's hard to find someone who doesn't love appetizers. ⚓ AND IT'S NO WONDER, because "apps" (as they're known in the restaurant industry) are specifically designed to be an exciting prelude to the meal that follows. If they're done right, they're made from colorful, flavorful ingredients with rich or intense flavors. They're designed to both ease your hunger and stimulate your anticipation of the coming repast. ⚓ APPETIZERS KNOW NO LIMITS. You can serve them as finger foods, or provide small plates and forks. There are simple appetizers that work well on buffets, and more complex and elegant dishes that are better suited to a seated meal. If you're serving a selection of apps, make sure to choose a range of colors and flavors. The beauty of making appetizers is that they often look and taste more complicated than they really are. ⚓ APPETIZERS ARE A GOOD WAY for the cook to play around with ingredients and cuisines to which he or she may not be accustomed. Everyone loves a little something exotic before a meal, so use your appetizer course as an opportunity to try out new things. How could anyone resist Bahama Mama Fritters with Tangy Caribbean Cocktail Sauce? Or Escargots Bourguignonne? For a party, offer your guests Mushroom Feuilletée: served warm, it's an elegant and absolutely smashing appetizer. ⚓ WHEN MY WIFE AND I ENTERTAIN, we often skip the main course altogether and opt instead for a "grazing" menu consisting of appetizers alone. In this chapter, you'll find six of our family's favorite appetizer recipes. Why not make a few and call it dinner?

SPLENDOUR OF
THE SEAS

chilled shrimp cocktail

SHRIMP is America's favorite shellfish. Most shrimp in the United States comes from bordering waters, notably the Atlantic and Pacific Oceans. Once cooked, the shells change color (either from pale pink to bright red or red to black). This is due to a heat caused chemical. There are different categories that shrimp fall into. These are: colossal, jumbo, extra-large, large, medium, small and miniature. For this recipe I suggest using large shrimp. Quite honestly, although good in flavor, smaller shrimp are too much of a hassle to peel. Shrimp can be found year round in most supermarkets or at your local seafood market.

Hot Cocktail Sauce

1/2 CUP (125 ML) CHILI SAUCE

1/2 CUP (125 ML) KETCHUP

6 TABLESPOONS GRATED FRESH HORSERADISH

4 TABLESPOONS WORCESTERSHIRE SAUCE

1 TEASPOON FRESH LEMON JUICE

TABASCO HOT PEPPER SAUCE TO TASTE

SALT AND FRESHLY GROUND BLACK PEPPER TO TASTE

ADD 2 TEASPOON COGNAC

In a nonreactive bowl, combine all the ingredients. Season to taste with salt and pepper. Cover and refrigerate until ready to use.

Shrimp

1/2 CUP (70 G) SHREDDED MESCLUN GREENS OR MIXED BABY LETTUCES

16 LARGE SHRIMP, PEELED, DEVEINED, BOILED AND CHILLED

4 CHERRY TOMATOES, CUT INTO WEDGES

4 LEMON WEDGES

8 WHOLE SALAD LEAVES FOR GARNISH, SUCH AS RED LEAF LETTUCE

4 SPRIGS DILL

Place the shredded greens in the bottom of 4 martini glasses. Place 4 shrimp on the rim of each glass and garnish decoratively with the tomato and lemon wedges, salad leaves and dill sprigs. Serve with the hot cocktail sauce.

Note: Although I suggest using martini glasses, a small plate may be used as well. Place the lettuce on the plate, followed by the shrimp in a circular fashion and top with the above garnishes. This, with the cocktail sauce served on the side, works just as well.

bahama mama fritters
with tangy caribbean cocktail sauce

FRITTERS ARE SMALL, sweet or savory, fried bits either made by combining chopped food with a thick batter or by dipping pieces of food into a similar batter. In this dish they are made from conch and cod. Conch is a mollusk that is encased in a brightly colored spiral shell and found mostly in the waters off of Florida and in the Caribbean. Summer is peak season for conch, which will most likely be available in Chinese, Italian or specialty fish markets. Conch should be stored tightly wrapped in the refrigerator for up to 2 days. Cod, on the other hand, is a popular saltwater fish found in the Pacific and North Atlantic Oceans. Its mild flavored meat is white, lean and firm. Cod can be found year round.

Cocktail Sauce

1/4 CUP (60 ML) FRESH LIME JUICE

2 CUPS (500 ML) KETCHUP

1 TABLESPOON WORCESTERSHIRE SAUCE

1/2 TABLESPOON PICKAPEPPA RED HOT SAUCE

SALT AND FRESHLY GROUND BLACK PEPPER TO TASTE

In a nonreactive bowl, combine all the ingredients. Cover and refrigerate until ready to use.

Fritters

1 1/2 CUPS (210 G) ALL-PURPOSE FLOUR

1 TABLESPOON BAKING POWDER

1/4 TEASPOON SALT

1/4 TEASPOON FRESHLY GROUND WHITE PEPPER

5 OUNCES (150 G) CONCH, COOKED AND FINELY CHOPPED

5 OUNCES (150 G) COD, COOKED AND FLAKED

3/4 CUP (200 ML) BOTTLED CLAM JUICE

1/2 CUP (125 ML) WHOLE MILK

1 1/2 QUARTS (1.5 L) PEANUT OR LIGHT OLIVE OIL

1 GREEN PLANTAIN

10 ROMAINE LETTUCE LEAVES, CLEANED AND DRIED

1 RED PEPPER, DICED SMALL

1. In a large bowl, combine the flour, baking powder, salt and pepper. In a medium bowl, combine the remaining ingredients except the oil. Make a well in the dry ingredients; add the wet ingredients and stir with a rubber spatula until just combined.

2. In a deep, heavy saucepan, heat half of the oil to 375°F/190°C. (To test the temperature, a small piece of bread dropped into the oil should float up to the surface almost immediately and brown within 45 seconds.)

3. Drop the fish mixture by spoonfuls into the oil. Deep-fry the fritters in batches until golden brown, for about 5 minutes. Transfer to a plate lined with paper towels to drain.

4. Peel and slice the plantain lengthwise as thinly as possible. In a deep, heavy saucepan, heat the remaining oil to 375°F/190°C. (Try the bread test again.) Carefully place the plantain strips into the oil, frying in batches so they do not stick to one another. With a slotted spoon move the strips around for about 1 minute until they become crisp. Immediately remove them and transfer to a plate lined with paper towels. Sprinkle with salt. (It is best to sprinkle them with salt while they are still warm so the salt will stick to them and take on the flavor.)

5. To serve the fritters, place a romaine lettuce leaf inside a bowl, along with a couple of the plantain strips. Placing them against the side of the bowl gives the dish a little height. Add about three fritters, sprinkle with diced red peppers and serve warm with Caribbean cocktail sauce on the side.

exotic fruit salad

YIELD: 4 SERVINGS

THIS FRUIT SALAD is very tropical in nature. Papaya is native to North America and is cultivated in semitropical zones around the world. It can range in size from 1 to 20 pounds (454 g-9 kg), with juicy and silky smooth flesh. The mango is sacred to India, the land of the fruit's origin. Similar to the papaya, it is exotically sweet and tart. Of course, you can always let your imagination run wild by using whatever fruits you like!

1/3 CUP (50 G) DICED FRESH RIPE PAPAYA

1/3 CUP (50 G) DICED FRESH RIPE MANGO

1/3 CUP (50 G) DICED HONEYDEW MELON

1/3 (50 G) CUP DICED CANTALOUPE

1/3 (50 G) CUP DICED SEEDLESS WATERMELON

8 STRAWBERRIES, WASHED AND QUARTERED LENGTHWISE

1/2 CUP (125 ML) PAPAYA NECTAR

1 TABLESPOON FRESH LIME JUICE

4 SLICES FRESH PINEAPPLE

8 PINEAPPLE LEAVES FOR GARNISH

4 MINT SPRIGS FOR GARNISH

In a nonreactive bowl, combine all the fruit. Add the papaya nectar and lime juice and toss to coat. Divide the salad among 4 chilled serving bowls and garnish each with 2 pineapple leaves and a mint sprig. Serve immediately.

mushroom feuilletée

EARLY GREEKS AND ROMANS are said to be among the first cultivators of mushrooms, using them in a wide array of dishes. Look for mushrooms that are firm, evenly colored with tightly closed caps. If all the gills are showing, they are past their prime. Avoid ones that are broken, damaged or have soft spots or a dark-tinged surface. Fresh mushrooms should be stored with cool air circulating around them. To clean them, brush with a damp paper towel. They should never be soaked because they will absorb water and become mushy.

Feuilletée (fwee-uh-tay) is a fancy French word for flaky or puff pastry. Once cooked, these thin, thin layers of dough will fluff up and double in size.

8 SQUARES PREPARED PUFF PASTRY, 3^1/$_2$ INCHES SQUARE (8.75 CM) (AVAILABLE FROM GOURMET FOOD STORES)

1 LARGE EGG, LIGHTLY BEATEN

1 STICK (120 G) UNSALTED BUTTER

2 MEDIUM SHALLOTS, CHOPPED

2 CLOVES GARLIC, CHOPPED

^{1}/$_2$ CUP (70 G) CHOPPED WHITE (ALSO KNOWN AS BUTTON) MUSHROOMS

^{1}/$_2$ CUP (70 G) CHOPPED CRIMINI MUSHROOMS

^{1}/$_2$ CUP (70 G) CHOPPED SHIITAKE MUSHROOMS, WITHOUT STEMS

^{1}/$_2$ CUP (70 G) CHOPPED OYSTER MUSHROOMS

SALT AND FRESHLY GROUND BLACK PEPPER TO TASTE

1 CUP (250 ML) DRY WHITE WINE

^{1}/$_2$ CUP (125 ML) HEAVY CREAM

^{1}/$_4$ CUP (60 ML) DEMI-GLACE (PAGE 149)

1 TEASPOON CHOPPED FRESH THYME LEAVES

CHOPPED FRESH PARSLEY FOR GARNISH

1. Preheat the oven to 375°F/190°C. Lightly coat a baking sheet with butter. Place the pastry squares on the baking sheet and brush with the beaten egg, taking care not to let the egg drip on the edges of the pastry. Bake for 15 to 20 minutes, or until golden and puffed. Transfer to a wire rack to cool. Reserve.

2. In a large sauté pan, heat the butter over medium heat. Add the shallots and cook, stirring, until softened and translucent, about 3 minutes. Add the garlic and mushrooms and sauté until most of the liquid is evaporated. Season with salt and pepper. With a slotted spoon, transfer the mushroom mixture to a bowl and reserve.

3. Add the wine, cream, demi-glace and thyme to any juices remaining in the pan and simmer for 3 minutes. Return the mushrooms to the pan and cook, stirring, until heated through. Adjust the seasonings to taste.

4. To serve, place a pastry square in the center of each of 4 warmed plates. Spoon some of the mushroom mixture on top. Place another pastry square on top and spoon the remaining mushrooms around the square. Sprinkle with chopped parsley and serve immediately.

Note: Feel free to use any combination of the mushrooms mentioned in the recipe. Portabello mushrooms may be used as well.

escargots bourguignonne

YIELD: 4 SERVINGS

ESCARGOTS are snails raised especially for the food service industry. Fresh snails are available year round and can be found in specialty markets. However, if you are like me, you are into convenience. That is why I suggest buying canned snails. They are easier to handle and can be found in most supermarkets.

A dish prepared *à la Bourguignonne* (boor-gee-nyon) means "in the style of Burgundy," one of France's best-known food areas. This region is located in the Eastern section of the country. Not only is this area known for its fabulous food, but it is also known for its fine red and white wines. Escargots Bourguignonne is the most famous dish to come from this area.

Garlic Butter

2 TABLESPOONS CHOPPED FRESH PARSLEY

2 CLOVES GARLIC, FINELY MINCED

1/2 TEASPOON DIJON MUSTARD

FRESHLY GROUND WHITE PEPPER TO TASTE

1 1/2 STICKS (180 G) UNSALTED BUTTER, SOFTENED

1/2 TEASPOON WORCESTERSHIRE SAUCE

1/2 TEASPOON COGNAC

Escargots

24 CANNED SNAILS, DRAINED

1 MEDIUM SHALLOT, FINELY CHOPPED

1 TABLESPOON DRY SHERRY

SALT TO TASTE

FRENCH BAGUETTE SLICES

1. For the garlic butter: in a food processor, combine the parsley, garlic and mustard. Season with white pepper. Process for 1 minute. Add 1 stick (120 g) butter, the Worcestershire sauce and cognac, and process for 2 minutes. Transfer the butter mixture to a small bowl and set aside.

2. For the snails: rinse the snails in a small colander under cold running water. Drain and pat dry with paper towels. In a sauté pan, heat the remaining 1/2 stick (60 g) butter over medium heat. Add the shallot and cook, stirring, until softened and translucent. Add the snails and sauté until completely heated through, about one minute. Stir in the sherry and season with salt and pepper. Remove from the heat and let cool.

3. Preheat the oven to 400°F/200°C. Transfer the snails to shells or to snail plates (if using the shells, divide them among 4 ovenproof dishes). Cover each snail completely with the reserved butter mixture.

4. Bake for a few minutes, or just until the snails are hot and the butter is completely melted and brown on top (do not overbake or the flavor of the butter will be compromised). Serve immediately with slices of the French baguette for dipping.

summer tomato
and buffalo mozzarella towers

THE TOMATO, like the eggplant and potato, is a member of the nightshade family. It is the fruit of the vine native to South America. There are many varieties available today. For this dish, I recommend using the beefsteak tomato. It has a meaty, hearty texture and it pairs well with the texture of the mozzarella. When choosing a tomato it should be firm, well shaped, free from blemishes and heavy for its size. Ripe tomatoes should be stored at room temperature and used within a few days.

Buffalo mozzarella is the most prized of the fresh mozzarella. It is made from a combination of water buffalo milk and cow's milk. This can be found in Italian markets, cheese shops and some supermarkets.

This is a perfect dish to serve when having company over. The presentation of this dish is what makes it so fascinating. It looks as though you have spent hours in the kitchen (because of the tower effect), but in reality takes less than 20 minutes to prepare. Try it, you will be amazed! This version of Summer Tomato and Buffalo Mozzarella Towers is served at our Portofino Restaurants, "The most romantic restaurants at sea."

4 MEDIUM-LARGE VINE-RIPENED TOMATOES, CUT INTO 1/4-INCH (6 MM) THICK SLICES

12 SLICES FRESH BUFFALO MOZZARELLA

1/2 CUP (125 ML) EXTRA-VIRGIN OLIVE OIL

3 1/2 TABLESPOONS BALSAMIC VINEGAR

FRESHLY GROUND BLACK PEPPER TO TASTE

8 FRESH BASIL LEAVES

Divide the tomato slices and mozzarella slices among 4 plates, stacking the slices like a tower on each plate and alternating the layers so that a tomato slice is on the bottom and also on the final layer on top. Drizzle the towers with the oil and balsamic vinegar. Sprinkle with the freshly ground pepper, and garnish each tower with 2 basil leaves. Serve immediately.

soups

No MATTER WHERE YOU GREW UP in the world, your childhood memories probably include watching your mother or grandmother stirring a kettle of soup. Soup is one of our most comforting foods, providing nourishment for mind, body and soul. And best of all, most soups can be prepared ahead of time, then chilled or reheated for serving. MAKING SOUP IS EASY and logical. Simply blend your choice of liquids with your favorite meats or seafood, your choice of carbohydrate (grains, beans, pasta, etc.) or vegetables or fruit. There's no better guide than your own good taste. And the results can be spectacular. But soup should be simple. Identify your main ingredient, cook it perfectly and then adjust the consistency. Cream tends to mute flavors, but it adds body and texture. Adding oils to soups can finish and enrich them. ACCORDING TO FRENCH MASTER CHEFS, soup is the "soul of the dinner." It can be served as a first course, or, in a formal meal, after the appetizer and before the fish. Soups can also be the focus around which a light lunch or dinner is formed. With a loaf of warm, crusty bread, a few greens and a bottle of wine, a bowl of warm soup makes a wonderful meal. Originally meant to be basic sustenance, soup has become one of our favorite year-round foods. THERE ARE THOUSANDS OF SOUPS out there, but they can generally be classified into four categories: broths, clear soups, thick soups and purées. MOST SOUPS continue to improve for a day or two after their initial cooking, and there's no reason you can't double any of these recipes and freeze the leftovers. Soups are one-pot meals that can be made on Sunday and served all week. SOUP IS SOMEHOW AS SATISFYING to prepare as it is to eat. It's a food that slows you down, warms you up, gives you fuel and reminds you of home, wherever your home may be. We all know that when you're sick, nothing—absolutely nothing—tastes as good as Chicken Noodle Soup. Some moms even swear it's better than penicillin for a cold or the flu. If there's any truth to that, I don't know, but I know it sure can't hurt! SOUP CAN BE ADAPTED for any mood or climate. As our cruise ships steam into sultry hot-weather ports, our guests crave our fabulous, fresh, chilled fruit and vegetable soups.

EXPLORER OF THE SEAS

beef consommé

A CONSOMMÉ is a rich, clear soup made by simmering broth or stock with a combination of ingredients known as a clarification. The combination of ingredients in the clarification— lean meat, egg whites, tomatoes or wine, and aromatic vegetables and herbs—removes any particles suspended in the broth. The clarification also helps fortify the soup's overall flavor.

The best quality consommés are crystal clear; completely fat free, amber in color, with a good body.

²/₃ POUND (300 G) GROUND BEEF

1 CUP (140 G) FINELY DICED ONION

²/₃ CUP (80 G) FINELY DICED CELERY

¹/₂ CUP (70 G) FINELY DICED CARROT

4 LARGE EGG WHITES

2 TABLESPOONS TOMATO PASTE

6 STEMS PARSLEY, CHOPPED

PINCH DRIED THYME

2 SMALL BAY LEAVES

2 CLOVES

¹/₄ TEASPOON CRUSHED BLACK PEPPERCORNS

3 ¹/₄ QUARTS (3.25 L) COLD BEEF STOCK (PAGE 151)

SALT AND FRESHLY GROUND BLACK PEPPER TO TASTE

8 STALKS CHIVES, CHOPPED

1. In a stockpot, combine all the ingredients except the beef stock, salt, freshly ground pepper and chives; mix well. Stir in about 2 cups (500 ml) of the cold beef stock and let stand for 30 minutes.

2. Gradually stir in the remaining cold beef stock, mixing well. Place the pot over moderately low heat and bring it to a simmer very slowly, stirring occasionally. Right when the mixture begins to simmer, stop stirring and reduce the heat. Simmer very slowly, uncovered, for 1¹/₂ hours, without stirring. Do not disturb the raft that forms.

3. Line a fine sieve with several layers of cheesecloth. Using a ladle, carefully strain the consommé through the sieve into a clean pot, taking care that the consommé does not become cloudy.

4. Spoon off any fat from the surface. Season with salt and pepper. To serve, ladle the consommé into warmed soup bowls and garnish with the chopped chives. Serve immediately.

Note: A great way to make fat-free stocks or consommés is to place the soup in the refrigerator overnight. The fat will rise to the top and it will solidify. This can be removed in one scoop, and *voila*, you have fat-free consommé or stock!

chicken gumbo

SOUPS

YIELD: 12 SERVINGS

THE NAME GUMBO is a derivation of the African word for "okra." This Creole specialty is a mainstay of New Orleans cuisine. It is a thick, stew-like dish that can have many ingredients, including vegetables such as okra, tomatoes and onions and one or several meats or shellfish such as chicken, sausage, ham, shrimp, crab or oysters. All good gumbos must begin with a dark roux, which adds a rich flavor. The roux is an equal mixture of flour and fat that is cooked over low heat and is used as a thickening agent.

For variations of this recipe, feel free to substitute the chicken for any shellfish or ham. It tastes just as great!

2 TABLESPOONS VEGETABLE OIL

2/3 CUP (85 G) CHOPPED ANDOUILLE SAUSAGE

1/2 POUND (225 G) RAW WHITE CHICKEN MEAT, CHOPPED

1 1/2 CUPS (210 G) CHOPPED ONION

1 LARGE GREEN BELL PEPPER, CORED, SEEDED AND CHOPPED (140 G)

1 1/4 CUPS (175 G) CHOPPED CELERY

1 LARGE JALAPEÑO PEPPER, CORED, SEEDED AND CHOPPED

1 1/2 CUPS (115 G) SPLIT AND SLICED SCALLIONS

2 TO 3 MEDIUM CLOVES GARLIC, CHOPPED

1 1/4 CUPS (175 G) SLICED OKRA (ABOUT 14 WHOLE)

2 RIPE MEDIUM TOMATOES, PEELED, SEEDED AND CHOPPED

1 CUP ALL-PURPOSE FLOUR (140 G), TOASTED IN THE OVEN ON A BAKING SHEET UNTIL DARK BROWN (NOT BLACK) IN COLOR

3 QUARTS (3 L) CHICKEN STOCK (SEE PAGE 152)

2 BAY LEAVES

1 TEASPOON DRIED OREGANO

1 TEASPOON DRIED ONION POWDER

1/2 TEASPOON DRIED THYME

1/2 TEASPOON DRIED BASIL

3 CUPS (420 G) RAW WHITE RICE, COOKED

1 TABLESPOON GUMBO FILÉ POWDER

SALT AND FRESHLY GROUND BLACK PEPPER TO TASTE

THYME SPRIGS FOR GARNISH

BASIL LEAVES FOR GARNISH

1. See Basic Knife Techniques (page 12) on how to concassé tomatoes.

2. In a large soup pot, heat the oil over medium-high heat. Add the sausage and chicken meat and cook, stirring, until the chicken loses its raw appearance. Add the onion, bell pepper, celery, jalapeño, scallions, garlic, okra and tomatoes. Sauté, stirring, until the vegetables become softened.

3. Add the flour and cook, stirring, for 2 minutes. Whisk in the chicken stock and bring to a boil. Stir to dissolve any lumps from the flour. Add the bay leaves, oregano, onion powder, thyme and basil. Reduce the heat and simmer, stirring occasionally, for 30 minutes.

4. Add the cooked rice and simmer, stirring, for 2 minutes. Remove from the heat and whisk in the filé powder. Season with salt and pepper. Divide the gumbo among warmed soup bowls, garnish with fresh thyme and basil and serve immediately.

cream of mushroom soup

5 TABLESPOONS UNSALTED
  BUTTER

1/3 CUP (50 G) FINELY CHOPPED
  ONION

1 MEDIUM CLOVE GARLIC,
  FINELY CHOPPED

3/4 POUND (340 G) FRESH WHITE
  MUSHROOMS, WIPED CLEAN
  AND LEFT WHOLE

1/2 CUP (125 ML) DRY
  WHITE WINE

2 CUPS (500 ML) CHICKEN STOCK
  (PAGE 152)

1 TABLESPOON ALL-PURPOSE
  FLOUR

1 CUP (250 ML) HEAVY CREAM

SALT AND FRESHLY GROUND
  BLACK PEPPER TO TASTE

1/2 POUND (225 G) FRESH WHITE
  MUSHROOMS, WIPED CLEAN
  AND SLICED

1/2 BUNCH CHIVES, CHOPPED

HERBED CROUTONS FOR GARNISH

1. In a medium saucepan, heat 2 tablespoons butter over medium-high heat. Add the onion and garlic and cook, stirring, until softened. Add the whole mushrooms and cook, stirring, for 2 to 3 minutes. Add the white wine and simmer until the liquid is reduced by half.

2. Add the chicken stock and bring to a boil. Reduce the heat and simmer, stirring occasionally, until the vegetables are very tender, about 10 to 15 minutes. Transfer the contents of the pan to a blender and purée until smooth. Return the soup to the pan and bring it to a simmer.

3. In a small bowl, mash 1-tablespoon butter with the flour. Whisk the flour paste into the simmering soup in increments, until the soup thickens slightly. Continue to simmer the soup, stirring, until no flour taste remains, about 10 minutes. Stir in the cream and return to a simmer. Season with salt and pepper and keep warm.

4. In a medium sauté pan, heat the remaining 2 tablespoons of butter over medium heat. Add the sliced mushrooms and cook, stirring, until lightly softened, about 5 to 7 minutes. To serve, divide the soup among warmed soup bowls. Garnish with the sliced mushrooms, chopped chives and croutons. Serve immediately.

Note: Please feel free to use any type of mushroom you choose.

split pea soup

YIELD: 10 SERVINGS

ALL PEAS are members of the legume family. Some, like the English Pea, are grown to be eaten fresh, while others like the Field Pea are grown to be dried. Please note that this recipe calls for the beans to be soaked overnight. Soaking allows the dried beans to absorb water, which allows them to begin dissolving the starches that can cause digestive discomfort. The traditional way of soaking the bean is to place 1 pound (454 g) of beans into a 5-quart (5 l) saucepan, covering them with 10 cups (1.8 l) of water. Cover and refrigerate for at least 6 hours. Drain and rinse them before using them in the soup.

2 TABLESPOONS VEGETABLE OIL

1/4 POUND (112 G) BACON, FINELY DICED

3/4 CUP (100 G) CHOPPED ONION

2/3 CUP (80 G) CHOPPED CARROT

1 CUP (140 G) CHOPPED CELERY (ABOUT 2 STALKS)

4 CLOVES GARLIC, FINELY MINCED

3 QUARTS (3 L) VEGETABLE STOCK OR WATER, COLD

1 POUND (454 G) SPLIT PEAS, PICKED OVER FOR STONES, COVERED IN 2 INCHES (5 CM) OF WATER AND SOAKED OVERNIGHT

2 HAM HOCKS, SMOKED

SALT AND FRESHLY GROUND WHITE PEPPER TO TASTE

2 SLICES OF BREAD

3 TABLESPOONS BUTTER, MELTED

1. In a large soup pot, heat the oil over medium heat. Add the bacon and cook, stirring, until crisp. Add the onion, carrot, celery and garlic. Cook, stirring constantly, until the vegetables soften and become translucent.

2. Add the stock or water, drained split peas and ham hocks. Bring the soup to a boil. Reduce the heat and simmer, stirring and skimming occasionally, until the peas and meat from the ham hocks are tender, about 2 hours. Remove the ham hocks and let them cool. Remove and chop the meat.

3. Strain the soup, reserving both solids and liquid. In a blender, puree the solids until smooth. Return the puree to the soup and simmer slowly for 10 minutes. Season with salt and pepper. To serve, divide the reserved ham hock meat among warmed soup bowls.

4. While the soup is cooking, you may prepare the croutons. Over low heat, melt the butter. Cut the bread into small cubes and toss with the butter, salt and pepper. Place on a baking tray and bake at 350° F/180°C for 15 minutes or until lightly browned. Ladle the soup over the meat and garnish with the croutons. Serve immediately.

Note: Feel free to use any type of bread to make the croutons.

chilled roasted peach soup

YIELD: 4 SERVINGS

THERE ARE TWO categories of peaches—freestone in which the stone or pit falls easily away from the flesh, and the clingstone, in which the fruit adheres stubbornly to the pit. Peaches are available from May to October in most regions of the United States. When choosing a peach, make sure it is intensely fragrant and it gives slightly to palm pressure. Since they bruise easily, make sure they do not have any soft spots.

4 RIPE LARGE PEACHES, PEELED, HALVED, AND PITTED

1$^{1}/_{2}$ CUPS (345 G) GRANULATED SUGAR

2 CUPS (500 ML) PEACH NECTAR, PLUS EXTRA IF NEEDED

1 STAR ANISE, CRACKED

1 VANILLA BEAN, SPLIT

JUICE OF 3 ORANGES

JUICE OF 2 LEMONS

$^{1}/_{2}$ PINT (150 G) STRAWBERRIES, GENTLY WASHED

2 SPRIGS FRESH MINT

1. Preheat the oven to 400°F/200°C. Lightly coat a baking sheet with butter. Place the peach halves; cut side down, on the prepared baking sheet. Sprinkle the peaches with $^{1}/_{2}$-cup (70 g) sugar and bake for 15 to 20 minutes, until well roasted.

2. Transfer the peaches to a food processor, along with any drippings from the baking sheet. Puree until smooth, stopping 2 or 3 times to scrape down the sides. Transfer to a large nonreactive bowl and set aside.

3. In a small nonreactive saucepan, combine the peach nectar, remaining sugar and star anise over medium heat. Use the tip of a blunt knife to scrape the vanilla bean seeds into the mixture. Bring to a boil and then remove from the heat. Let the syrup infuse for about 1 hour in a warm place. Strain through a fine sieve into a nonreactive bowl and add the citrus juices.

4. Tasting as you go, slowly add the peach syrup to the peach purée until the desired flavor is achieved. If the soup is nicely flavored but too thick, thin it with a little plain peach juice. Cover and refrigerate until completely cold.

5. To serve, ladle the soup into chilled soup plates or cups and garnish with the sliced strawberries and mint sprigs.

chilled red berry soup

soups

YIELD: 4 TO 6 SERVINGS

1 PINT (150 G) FRESH
RASPBERRIES, GENTLY WASHED

1 PINT (150 G) FRESH
STRAWBERRIES, GENTLY
WASHED AND TRIMMED

2 CUPS (500 ML) SOUR CREAM

1 CUP (250 ML) WHOLE MILK

1 CUP (250 ML) GINGER ALE

1/4 CUP (60 G) GRANULATED
SUGAR

2 TABLESPOONS TRIPLE SEC

2 TABLESPOONS FRESH
LEMON JUICE

FRESH MINT LEAVES FOR GARNISH

1. Reserve 6 of the strawberries and 12 of the raspberries for
garnish. In a blender or food processor combine the remaining
berries and purée until smooth. Strain the mixture through a
fine sieve over a nonreactive bowl, pushing through as much of
the pulp as you can, leaving the seeds behind.

2. Whisk the remaining ingredients, except the reserved berries
and mint, into the purée. Cover and refrigerate until cold. To
serve, divide the soup among chilled soup bowls and garnish with
the reserved berries and mint leaves.

Note: This is a great soup to serve during those hot summer days
that we all love!

chilled apricot soup

YIELD: 6 SERVINGS

THIS FRUIT of ancient lineage
has been grown in China for
over 4000 years. It now can
be grown in most temperature
climates, with California producing over 90 percent of the
American crop. A relative of the
peach, it is smaller and has a
smooth, oval pit that falls out
easily when the fruit is halved.
Dried apricots have already
been pitted and peeled, and
most of their moisture has
been removed. Apricots are a
good source of vitamin A, iron
and calcium.

20 FRESH MEDIUM APRICOTS
(AROUND 5 CUPS, DICED)
(700 G)

1 CUP (250 ML) CLUB SODA

1 CUP (250 ML) DRY
WHITE WINE

1/2 CUP (70 G)
GRANULATED SUGAR

JUICE OF 1 LEMON

1/3 CUP (75 ML) COGNAC

WHIPPED CREAM AND CHOPPED
FRESH MINT FOR GARNISH

1. In a medium saucepan, bring 2 quarts (2 l) water to a boil.
Working in batches, plunge the apricots in the boiling water and
leave them in just until the skins are loosened, 10 to 20 seconds.
With a slotted spoon, transfer the apricots to a large bowl of cold
water to cool. Slip off the skins and cut the apricots in half.
Remove the pits and dice the apricots.

2. In a large nonreactive bowl, combine the apricots, club soda,
wine, sugar, lemon juice and cognac. Ladle the mixture in batches
into a blender and purée until smooth. Transfer the soup to another
bowl. Cover and refrigerate. To serve, divide the soup among
chilled soup bowls and garnish with whipped cream and mint.

chilled washington apple soup

THE GOLDEN DELICIOUS APPLE has a midly sweet flavor and is juicy with a crisp flesh that resists browning.

In case you do not want to peel and chop 18 apples, you may go ahead and use apple-sauce instead. Substitute 16 ounces (500 ml) of applesauce for the apples. If applesauce is being used, all you have to do is combine everything except the ice cream in the blender and purée until smooth. Once it is smooth, blend in the ice cream and serve.

6 CUPS (1.5 L) WATER

JUICE OF 2 LEMONS

4 TABLESPOONS GRANULATED SUGAR

1/2 TEASPOON GROUND CINNAMON, PLUS EXTRA FOR GARNISH

18 GOLDEN DELICIOUS APPLES, PEELED, CORED AND ROUGHLY DICED

4 CUPS (560 G) VANILLA ICE CREAM

1. In a large nonreactive saucepan, combine all the ingredients except the ice cream. Bring the mixture to a boil. Reduce the heat and simmer, covered, until the apples are soft.

2. Transfer the soup in batches to a blender and purée until smooth. Strain the soup through a fine sieve into a nonreactive bowl. Let cool to room temperature. Cover and refrigerate until cold, about 4 hours. To serve, stir in the ice cream and divide the soup among chilled soup bowls. Sprinkle with cinnamon and serve immediately.

chilled pineapple soup

FRESH PINEAPPLE is available year round with a peak season from March to July. This fruit must be picked ripe because the starch will not convert to sugar once it has been removed from the plant. Choose pineapples that are slightly soft to the touch with a strong, full color and no sign of greening. The leaves should be crisp and green with no yellow or brown tips. Refrigerate fresh pineapple tightly wrapped for up to three days.

2 POUNDS (905 G) CHOPPED FRESH RIPE PINEAPPLE

2 CUPS (280 G) SOUR CREAM

1 CUP (250 ML) WHOLE MILK

1 CUP (250 ML) GINGER ALE

1 CUP (140 G) GRANULATED SUGAR

2 TEASPOONS PURE VANILLA EXTRACT

2 TABLESPOONS FRESH LEMON JUICE

1/4 CUP (35 G) UNSWEETENED FLAKED COCONUT

1. In a nonreactive bowl, combine all the ingredients except the coconut. Transfer the mixture in batches to a food processor and purée until smooth. Pour the soup into a clean nonreactive bowl. Cover and refrigerate until cold.

2. Meanwhile, toast the coconut: In a dry skillet over high heat, toss or stir the coconut, taking care not to scorch it, until lightly browned. To serve, divide the cold soup among chilled soup bowls and garnish with the coconut.

mangospacho

MANGOS are fruits with extremely juicy, fragrant flesh, and are exotically sweet and tart. They are in season from May to September. When picked, they should be unblemished, with a yellow skin that is blushed with red. The only negative to this fruit is the huge, flat seed that traverses its length. The fruit must be carefully carved away from the seed with a sharp knife.

By now, after reading this, I would be saying to myself, forget it. It is not worth it. Wrong! Go ahead and buy canned mango. It works just as well in this recipe and can be found year round in supermarkets everywhere. This recipe should not be missed, it is a great alternative to the gazpacho everyone is used to.

8 CUPS (1 KG) PEELED AND FINELY DICED MANGO (ABOUT 12 MANGOS)

1 CUP (250 ML) WATER

1 CUP (250 ML) GINGER ALE

1/2 CUP (125 ML) RICE WINE VINEGAR

1/2 CUP (125 ML) LIGHT OLIVE OIL

1 TABLESPOON GRANULATED SUGAR

SALT AND FRESHLY GROUND BLACK PEPPER TO TASTE

2 CUCUMBERS, PEELED, SEEDED AND FINELY DICED

1/2 CUP (70 G) FINELY DICED RED ONION

3/4 CUP (100 G) CHOPPED FRESH CILANTRO

1. In a blender or food processor, combine half the mango with the water, ginger ale, vinegar, oil and sugar. Purée until smooth. Season with salt and pepper. Transfer the soup to a nonreactive bowl. Cover and refrigerate until cold, about 4 hours.

2. In another nonreactive bowl, combine the remaining 4 cups (560 g) mango, cucumber, red onion and 1/2 cup (70 g) cilantro. Cover and refrigerate until cold.

3. To serve, divide the cucumber mixture among chilled soup bowls that are each sitting in a bowl of crushed ice. Ladle the soup over the cucumber mixture and sprinkle with the remaining 1/4 cup (35 g) cilantro. Serve immediately.

salads and salad dressings

WHEN I WAS GROWING UP, "salad" was important to my mother who was a chef. We grew our own lettuce, tomatoes and cucumbers, but the choice was limited. How far we've come! Thanks to the continuing efforts of a growing network of small farmers, organic and otherwise, today we have an amazing array of fresh greens and other goodies from which we can make sensational salads year round at our fingertips. ⚓ THE DEFINITION of what makes a salad has also expanded considerably and salads are now fertile testing ground for inventive new culinary ideas. ⚓ GREENS are at their best when just picked from the garden, so look for vibrant colors, firm leaves and a pleasing fragrance as you shop. Consider mixing lettuces that are sweet and delicately flavored with others, such as arugula, that are far more assertive. Bitter greens add a nice bite. ⚓ TWO OF THE SALADS, Cobb and Caesar, were invented by famous restaurateurs. It was July 4, 1924, for instance, when Caesar Cardini, the owner of an Italian restaurant called Caesar's Palace, in Tijuana, Mexico, had a group of guests from California arrive at the door. Cardini had little food in the pantry. Rather than turn them away, however, he improvised a salad using what he had on hand: eggs, romaine lettuce, dry bread, Parmesan cheese, garlic, olive oil, lemon juice and, of course, pepper. Voila—a classic was born! Today this salad is served worldwide with scores of variations, the most popular being the addition of anchovies. ⚓ WHEN MAKING VINAIGRETTES, always use your best olive oil and vinegar. Their complex aromas and fruity flavors will shine, not having been broken down by cooking. When tasting your vinaigrette, its best to dip something into it, a component of your salad, even just a lettuce leaf. Dress your greens after they have been washed, dried and chilled. ⚓

MAJESTY OF THE SEAS

AT HOME—and in restaurant kitchens as well—I often see lettuces that have not been dried properly. Make sure to use a salad spinner; if you don't have one, try this clever method I learned from a fellow chef: wrap the greens in a clean bath towel and whirl it over your head. The greens will be spun dry within a minute or two. ⚓ OVER THE YEARS, I've learned to dress and toss salad in one easy step. Put your dressing in the bowl then add your salad. Then simply use your hands, picking up a bit of the dressing with each turn. This lets you determine how much dressing each leaf gets and it leaves the lettuce un-bruised.

cobb salad

A RESTAURANT in Hollywood, California called the Brown Derby made this salad popular in the mid-1900s. It usually consists of chopped chicken or turkey, bacon, hard cooked eggs, tomatoes, avocado, cheddar cheese, lettuce and some type of blue or Roquefort cheese.

Vinaigrette

1/2 CUP (125 ML) RED WINE VINEGAR

1 TABLESPOON FRESH LEMON JUICE

1 1/2 TABLESPOONS DIJON MUSTARD

1 1/2 CUPS (375 ML) EXTRA-VIRGIN OLIVE OIL

SALT AND FRESHLY GROUND BLACK PEPPER TO TASTE

In a nonreactive bowl, combine the vinegar, lemon juice, and mustard. Slowly whisk in the oil. Season with salt and pepper. Cover and refrigerate until ready to use.

To Assemble

1 1/2 POUNDS (679 G) BONELESS, SKINLESS CHICKEN BREAST

2 OUNCES (57 G) VEGETABLE OIL

SALT AND FRESHLY GROUND BLACK PEPPER TO TASTE

4 MEDIUM TOMATOES, PEELED, SEEDED AND
CUT IN 1/2 INCH (1.25 CM) DICE

1 LARGE HEAD ROMAINE, CHICORY, OR RED LEAF LETTUCE,
WASHED AND DRIED

4 LARGE HARD-COOKED EGGS, CUT INTO 1/2-INCH (1.25 CM) DICE

2 AVOCADOS, PEELED, PITTED, AND CUT INTO 1/2-INCH (1.25 CM) DICE

1/2 POUND (225 G) BLUE CHEESE, CRUMBLED INTO LARGE PIECES

1 POUND (454 G) BACON, COOKED CRISP AND BROKEN INTO LARGE PIECES

1 CUP (140 G) SCALLIONS, CUT INTO 1/2-INCH (1.25 CM) PIECES

1. Heat a charcoal grill to medium hot. Season the chicken with salt and pepper and brush with the oil. Grill lightly on both sides until well marked but still moist inside. (Alternatively, broil for 8 minutes.) Let cool. Cut into 1/2-inch (1.25 CM) dice, cover, and refrigerate until ready to use.

2. See Basic Knife Techniques (page 12) for how to concassé tomatoes.

3. Tear the lettuce into small pieces and divide among 4 chilled plates. Top with the chicken. Attractively arrange the tomatoes, eggs, avocados, blue cheese and bacon in individual piles around the lettuce. Sprinkle the scallions over the chicken. Serve with the vinaigrette on the side.

classic tomato salad

1 POUND (454 G) FIRM, RIPE
BEEFSTEAK TOMATOES

1 TEASPOON GRANULATED SUGAR

SALT AND FRESHLY GROUND
BLACK PEPPER TO TASTE

6 TABLESPOONS EXTRA-VIRGIN
OLIVE OIL

2 TABLESPOONS WHITE WINE
VINEGAR

1 TABLESPOON RED ONION,
CHOPPED FINE

1 TABLESPOON CHOPPED FRESH
CHIVES OR PARSLEY

1. Slice the tomatoes into quarters and arrange them on a serving plate. Sprinkle the tomatoes with the sugar. Season with salt and pepper.

2. In a small nonreactive bowl, combine the oil and vinegar. Add the basil, diced red onion, salt and pepper. Spoon the mixture over the tomatoes. Cover the salad with plastic wrap and refrigerate for at least one hour. When ready to serve, toss everything together. This will help distribute the marinade. Place in a chilled bowl and sprinkle with chives or parsley before serving.

Note: I suggest using beefsteak tomatoes for this recipe, however, quartered plum tomatoes may be used as well.

cedar key salad

YIELD: 4 TO 6 SERVINGS

Florida Orange Dressing

1 CUP (250 ML) PREPARED OR BASIC MAYONNAISE
(PAGE 53)

1 CLOVE GARLIC, CRUSHED

1 TABLESPOON HONEY

1 TABLESPOON DIJON MUSTARD

2 TABLESPOONS EXTRA-VIRGIN OLIVE OIL

1/4 CUP (60 ML) ORANGE JUICE CONCENTRATE

1 TABLESPOON GRATED ORANGE ZEST

2 TABLESPOONS FINELY CHOPPED FRESH PARSLEY

SALT AND FRESHLY GROUND BLACK PEPPER TO TASTE

In a nonreactive bowl, combine all the ingredients. Cover and refrigerate until ready to use.

To Assemble

1/2 HEAD ROMAINE OR ICEBERG LETTUCE,
WASHED, DRIED AND CHOPPED

1/2 POUND (275 G) FRESH PINEAPPLE,
FINELY DICED

1 15-OUNCE (425 G) CAN HEARTS OF PALM,
DRAINED AND SLICED

1 MEDIUM RED BELL PEPPER, CORED, SEEDED
AND DICED

4 TABLESPOONS CHOPPED FRESH CHIVES

Divide the lettuce among chilled salad plates. In a large bowl, combine the remaining ingredients and spoon them over the lettuce. Serve with Florida Orange Dressing on the side.

cucumber and dill salad

salads

THOUGHT TO BE A GOOD LUCK SYMBOL, dill has been around for thousands of years. This annual herb is marketed in both fresh and dried forms. Since fresh dill loses its fragrance during heating, it is should be added toward the end of cooking.

1 LARGE CUCUMBER, PEELED, HALVED LENGTHWISE, SEEDED, AND CUT INTO HALF MOONS

SALT TO TASTE

4 TABLESPOONS FRESH LEMON JUICE OR WHITE WINE VINEGAR

FRESHLY GROUND BLACK PEPPER TO TASTE

1 TABLESPOON CHOPPED FRESH DILL

Place the cucumber in a colander and sprinkle with a little salt. Let stand for 30 minutes. Rinse, pat dry on paper towels and transfer to a nonreactive bowl. Sprinkle with the lemon juice or vinegar and season with salt and pepper. Stir in the dill and serve immediately.

greek salad

TRADITIONALLY I like to make this dish during those summer months when it is too hot to cook. It takes less than 30 minutes to prepare and it is a nice hearty yet healthy salad. Served either on a platter or in a large bowl, I know everyone will love it. I like to serve this with warmed pita bread and extra lemon dressing to dunk the pita in!

Lemon Dressing

3 TABLESPOONS FRESH LEMON JUICE

1/2 CUP (125 ML) EXTRA-VIRGIN OLIVE OIL

SALT AND FRESHLY GROUND BLACK PEPPER TO TASTE

To Assemble

1/2 HEAD ROMAINE LETTUCE, WASHED, DRIED AND CHOPPED

1 CUP (140 G) SHREDDED SPINACH LEAVES

3 PLUM TOMATOES, CUT INTO QUARTERS

1/2 CUCUMBER, PEELED, HALVED LENGTHWISE, SEEDED AND SLICED

1/2 WHITE ONION, THINLY SLICED INTO RINGS

1 MEDIUM GREEN BELL PEPPER, CORED, SEEDED AND SLICED

12 KALAMATA OLIVES, PITTED

6 OUNCES (170 G) FETA CHEESE, CUBED

1 TEASPOON CHOPPED FRESH OREGANO OR MARJORAM

Place the lemon juice in a small nonreactive bowl. Slowly whisk in the oil. Season with salt and pepper. Cover and refrigerate until ready to use.

In a large nonreactive serving bowl, combine the lettuce and spinach. Add the tomatoes, cucumber, onion and bell pepper, and toss to combine. Arrange the olives and cheese on top and drizzle with the lemon dressing. Sprinkle with the oregano or marjoram and serve immediately.

curried rice salad

YIELD: 10 SIDE-DISH SERVINGS

salads

THIS IS A GREAT DISH to serve at a party, as it will add vibrant color to your buffet table. Your guests will love it!

2 POUNDS (905 G) LONG-GRAIN BROWN RICE

1/2 CUP (70 G) CHOPPED DRIED APRICOTS

3 TABLESPOONS SUNFLOWER OIL

1/2 CUP (70 G) UNSALTED CASHEWS

1 MEDIUM ONION, CHOPPED

1 TEASPOON CUMIN SEEDS

2 TABLESPOONS CURRY POWDER

6 TABLESPOONS ORANGE JUICE

2 TABLESPOONS RAISINS

SALT AND FRESHLY GROUND BLACK PEPPER TO TASTE

CHOPPED FRESH CILANTRO FOR GARNISH

1. Cook the rice according to the package instructions. Meanwhile, place the apricots in a small bowl and add enough boiling water to cover. Let soak for 10 minutes; drain.

2. In a skillet, heat the oil over medium-high heat. Add the cashews and toss or stir them, taking care not to scorch them, until lightly browned. With a slotted spoon, transfer them to a plate lined with paper towels to drain. Set aside.

3. Reduce the heat to medium and add the onion to the skillet. Cook, stirring, for 3 to 4 minutes. Stir in the cumin seeds and curry powder and cook for 2 minutes. Pour in the orange juice and simmer for 1 minute more. Remove from the heat.

4. When the rice is cooked, transfer it to a nonreactive bowl. Add the warm orange juice mixture and toss to coat. Stir in the drained apricots, cashews and raisins. Season with salt and pepper. Let the salad stand for at least 2 hours before serving. Garnish with chopped cilantro.

grilled new potato
and asparagus salad

NEW POTATOES are simply young potatoes (any variety) that have not had time to convert their sugar fully into starch. Because of this, they have a crisp, waxy texture and thin, undeveloped waxy skins. New potatoes are small enough to cook whole and are excellent boiled or pan-roasted. Because they retain their shape after being cooked, they are well suited to be used in potato salad.

When buying the potatoes, look for ones that are firm. They should not have wrinkles, sprouts or cracks. Store potatoes in a cool, dark, well ventilated place for up to 2 weeks. New potatoes should be used within 3 days of purchase.

2 POUNDS (905 G) MEDIUM-SIZE NEW POTATOES, SCRUBBED AND QUARTERED

3 TABLESPOONS PURE OLIVE OIL

2 TEASPOONS MINCED GARLIC

SALT AND FRESHLY GROUND BLACK PEPPER TO TASTE

VEGETABLE OIL SPRAY

1 POUND (454 G) MEDIUM ASPARAGUS, TRIMMED

1/4 CUP (35 G) CHOPPED RED ONION

1/4 CUP (35 G) CHOPPED SCALLIONS

1/4 CUP (35 G) OIL-PACKED SUN-DRIED TOMATOES, DRAINED AND CHOPPED

2 TEASPOONS FINELY CHOPPED FRESH BASIL

1. Heat a covered charcoal or gas grill to medium hot. In a large bowl, combine the potatoes, 2 tablespoons oil and garlic. Toss to coat. Season with salt and pepper. Spray the grill with vegetable oil spray and place the potatoes on the grill. Cook, until lightly browned and tender when pierced with a fork, about 15 minutes. (Turn several times with a spatula for even cooking.) Transfer the potatoes to a large serving bowl and tent loosely with aluminum foil to keep warm.

2. Prepare a bowl of ice water and set aside. Bring 2 quarts (2 l) of salted water to a boil. Once the water has reached a boil, place the asparagus in the pot and let them cook for about 5 minutes or until they turn bright green in color. Immediately shock them in the ice water. Once cold, drain and dry the asparagus.

3. Toss the asparagus with the remaining 1 tablespoon oil. Season with salt and pepper. Lay the asparagus on the grill perpendicular to the long grids (so they don't fall through the grill) and turn often with tongs until softened and tinged brown. Transfer to a cutting board and cut each into 3 to 4 diagonal pieces. Add to the potatoes along with the remaining ingredients. Toss to combine. Adjust the seasonings and serve immediately.

pasta, shrimp and salmon salad

PASTA, SHRIMP AND SALMON are definitely a combination that should not be missed. I serve it often to my family and they love it. Although I suggest using shell pasta for this dish, remember the possibilities are endless. Other pastas that go well with shrimp and salmon include: fettuccine, bowtie, rigatoni and macaroni. Please remember to let your imagination run wild when it comes to trying this dish!

1/2 POUND (225 G) DRIED SMALL PASTA SHELLS (YOU MAY USE SPINACH SHELLS IF DESIRED)

1 1/2 TABLESPOONS FRESH LEMON JUICE

1 1/2 TABLESPOONS TOMATO JUICE

1 1/2 TABLESPOONS CHOPPED FRESH PARSLEY

1 1/2 TABLESPOONS CHOPPED FRESH TARRAGON

4 1/4 TABLESPOONS EXTRA-VIRGIN OLIVE OIL

SALT AND FRESHLY GROUND BLACK PEPPER TO TASTE

3/4 POUND (340 G) MEDIUM SHRIMP, COOKED, PEELED AND DEVEINED

1/4 POUND (120 G) SMOKED SALMON, CUT INTO THIN STRIPS

2 PLUM TOMATOES, QUARTERED

CHOPPED AND WHOLE CHIVES FOR GARNISH

1. Cook the pasta in a stockpot of boiling salted water until *al dente*, 6 to 8 minutes. Drain, rinse with cold water and drain again. Drizzle with a bit of olive oil to prevent sticking. Set aside.

2. For the dressing: In a small nonreactive bowl, combine the lemon juice, tomato juice, parsley and tarragon. Slowly whisk in the oil. Season with salt and pepper.

3. In a large bowl, combine the pasta and dressing. Toss to coat. Add the shrimp and salmon and toss until all the ingredients are well incorporated. Transfer to a serving bowl. Place the quartered tomatoes around the edge of the bowl. Garnish with chopped chives and a bunch of whole chives placed on top. Serve immediately.

salad niçoise

NIÇOISE is a French phrase that means "as prepared in Nice," typifying the cuisine found in and around that French Riviera city. This cooking style is identified with hot and cold dishes that include the integral ingredients of tomatoes, black olives and anchovies. Salad Niçoise contains these basic ingredients plus French green beans, onions, tuna, hard-cooked eggs and herbs.

Vinaigrette

1 TABLESPOON RED WINE VINEGAR

1 TABLESPOON FRESH LEMON JUICE

1/4 TEASPOON DIJON MUSTARD

1/4 CUP (60 ML) EXTRA-VIRGIN OLIVE OIL

1/4 TEASPOON GRANULATED SUGAR

SALT AND FRESHLY GROUND BLACK PEPPER TO TASTE

To Assemble

1/4 POUND (112 G) HARICOTS VERTS (THIN GREEN BEANS), ENDS TRIMMED

6 SMALL TOMATOES, QUARTERED

1/2 CUCUMBER, PEELED, HALVED LENGTHWISE, SEEDED AND DICED

1 MEDIUM RED BELL PEPPER, CORED, SEEDED AND SLICED

6 SCALLIONS, CHOPPED

1 6-OUNCE (170 G) CAN TUNA, DRAINED AND FLAKED

1/2 CUP (70 G) RIPE OLIVES (PREFERABLY NIÇOISE), PITTED

1 TABLESPOON CHOPPED FRESH PARSLEY

3 LARGE HARD-COOKED EGGS, QUARTERED

1 2-OUNCE (57 G) CAN ANCHOVY FILLETS, DRAINED

SALT AND FRESHLY GROUND PEPPER TO TASTE

FRESH BASIL LEAVES FOR GARNISH

In a nonreactive bowl, combine the vinegar, lemon juice, sugar and mustard. Slowly whisk in the oil. Season with salt and pepper. Cover and refrigerate until ready to use.

1. Prepare a bowl of ice water. Bring a medium saucepan of salted water to a boil. Add the haricots verts and cook just until bright green and tender-crisp, about 3 minutes. Remove the haricots verts with a strainer and shock them in the ice water to stop the cooking. Drain and cut into 1/2-inch (1.25 cm) lengths.

2. In a large salad bowl, combine the haricots verts, tomatoes, cucumber, bell pepper, scallions, tuna and olives. Toss to combine. Add the vinaigrette and the parsley; toss to coat. Season to taste with salt and pepper. Arrange the eggs on top of the salad. Cut the anchovy fillets in half lengthwise and make a crisscross pattern on the salad. Garnish with basil leaves and serve immediately.

spinach salad
with bacon dressing

Bacon Dressing

1 SLICE, LEAN BACON

1/2 CUP (125 ML) WHITE WINE VINEGAR

5 TEASPOONS MINCED SHALLOTS

1/2 TEASPOON MINCED GARLIC

1/2 TEASPOON DIJON MUSTARD

1 TEASPOON BROWN SUGAR

1/4 TEASPOON FRESHLY CHOPPED THYME

1 CUP (250 ML) VEGETABLE OIL

SALT AND FRESHLY GROUND PEPPER TO TASTE

In a skillet, cook the bacon until crisp on both sides. With a slotted spoon, transfer the bacon to a nonreactive bowl. Add the garlic and shallots to the rendered bacon fat and sweat. Blend in the brown sugar and melt. Transfer to the bowl with the bacon in it. While still warm, add the vinegar, fresh thyme and the mustard. Slowly whisk in the oil. Season with salt and pepper.

To Assemble

6 CUPS (840 G) YOUNG SPINACH LEAVES

1 SMALL RED ONION, THINLY SLICED

4 LARGE WHITE MUSHROOMS, WIPED CLEAN AND SLICED

SALT AND FRESHLY GROUND BLACK PEPPER TO TASTE

2 LARGE HARD-COOKED EGGS, CHOPPED

In a salad bowl, combine the spinach, onion and mushrooms. Toss the spinach mixture with just enough bacon dressing to lightly coat the ingredients. Top with the chopped eggs and serve immediately.

traditional caesar salad

YIELD: 4 SERVINGS

THIS SALAD is said to have been created in 1924 by Italian chef Caesar Cardini who owned a restaurant in Tijuana, Mexico. It consists of greens (classically romaine lettuce), tossed with garlic vinaigrette dressing, grated Parmesan cheese, coddled eggs, croutons and sometimes anchovies.

Caesar Dressing

4 CLOVES GARLIC

3 TABLESPOONS FRESH LEMON JUICE

6 ANCHOVY FILLETS, DRAINED, OR 2 TEASPOONS ANCHOVY PASTE

2 TABLESPOONS DIJON MUSTARD

2 TEASPOONS WORCESTERSHIRE SAUCE

2 LARGE EGG YOLKS

SALT TO TASTE

1 CUP (250 ML) EXTRA-VIRGIN OLIVE OIL

In a blender, combine all the ingredients except the oil. Blend until smooth, about 2 minutes. With the motor running, slowly add the oil. Adjust the seasoning. Transfer to a container. Cover and refrigerate until ready to use.

To Assemble

3 TABLESPOONS EXTRA-VIRGIN OLIVE OIL

1 CUP (140 G) CUBED CRUSTLESS SOURDOUGH BREAD

SALT AND FRESHLY GROUND BLACK PEPPER TO TASTE

2 HEADS ROMAINE LETTUCE, WASHED AND DRIED

1 1/2 CUPS (210 G) SHAVED OR GRATED PARMESAN CHEESE

1. Preheat the oven to 375°F/190°C. Coat a baking sheet with the oil. Add the bread cubes and toss to coat. Season with salt and pepper. Bake for 8 to 10 minutes, or until golden brown. Transfer to a plate lined with paper towels to drain. Reserve.

2. Tear the romaine into bite-size pieces and place in a large salad bowl. Add just enough Caesar dressing to coat the lettuce. Divide the salad among 4 chilled plates and top with the Parmesan and croutons. Serve immediately.

Royal Culinary Collections[TM] Galley Caesar Salad Dressing will enhance your salad.

basic mayonnaise

A THICK, creamy dressing that is an emulsion of oil, egg yolks, lemon juice or vinegar and seasonings. If egg yolks are not used, the product is called salad dressing, which is also sweeter than mayonnaise. All mayonnaise should be refrigerated once made or opened. Freshly made is far superior in taste and texture and should only be stored for 3 to 4 days. The commercial mayonnaise can be stored for up to 6 months.

2 LARGE EGG YOLKS

1 TEASPOON DIJON MUSTARD

SALT AND FRESHLY GROUND BLACK PEPPER TO TASTE

WORCESTERSHIRE SAUCE TO TASTE

1 1/2 CUPS (375 ML) EXTRA-VIRGIN OLIVE OIL

1 TABLESPOON FRESH LEMON JUICE

In a food processor, combine the egg yolks and mustard. Blend until smooth. Season with salt, pepper and Worcestershire sauce. With the motor running, add the oil very, very slowly through the feed tube, stopping once or twice to scrape down the sides. The mixture should become very thick. Add the lemon juice and blend until incorporated. Adjust the seasonings. Transfer to a container. Cover and refrigerate until ready to use.

garlic mayonnaise

YIELD: 2 CUPS (500 ML)

8 MEDIUM CLOVES GARLIC

2 LARGE EGG YOLKS, LIGHTLY BEATEN

3 TABLESPOONS FRESH LEMON JUICE

1 TEASPOON DIJON MUSTARD

1 1/2 CUPS (375 ML) EXTRA-VIRGIN OLIVE OIL

SALT AND FRESHLY GROUND WHITE PEPPER TO TASTE

In a food processor, chop the garlic cloves. Add the egg yolks, lemon juice and mustard. Blend until smooth. With the motor running, add the oil very, very slowly through the feed tube, stopping once or twice to scrape down the sides. The mixture should become very thick. Season with salt and pepper. If necessary thin with reserved liquid. Transfer to a container. Cover and refrigerate until ready to use.

classic vinaigrette

ONE OF THE FIVE "mother sauces," vinaigrette is a basic oil-and-vinegar combination, generally used to dress salad greens and other cold vegetable, meat or fish dishes. In its simplest form, it consists of oil, vinegar (usually 3 parts oil to 1 part vinegar), salt and pepper. More elaborate variations can include any of various ingredients such as spices, herbs, shallots, onions, mustard, etc.

- 4 TABLESPOONS RED WINE VINEGAR
- 4 TABLESPOONS FRESH LEMON JUICE
- 1 TEASPOON DIJON MUSTARD
- 2 TEASPOONS GRANULATED SUGAR
- 1 CUP (250 ML) EXTRA-VIRGIN OLIVE OIL
- SALT AND FRESHLY GROUND BLACK PEPPER TO TASTE

In a nonreactive bowl, combine the vinegar, lemon juice, mustard and sugar. Slowly whisk in the oil. Season with salt and pepper. Cover and refrigerate until ready to use.

garlic vinaigrette

- 6 CLOVES GARLIC, CRUSHED
- SALT TO TASTE
- PEPPER TO TASTE
- 3 TABLESPOONS WHITE WINE VINEGAR
- 3/4 TEASPOON DIJON MUSTARD
- 2 TABLESPOONS FRESH LEMON JUICE
- 3/4 CUP (200 ML) EXTRA-VIRGIN OLIVE OIL

In a wooden salad bowl, combine the garlic and salt. With the back of a wooden spoon, crush the garlic with the salt until a paste forms. Stir in the vinegar, mustard and lemon juice. Slowly whisk in the oil. Season with salt and pepper. Cover and refrigerate until ready to use.

ginger vinaigrette

- 1/2 CUP (125 ML) SOY SAUCE
- 1/2 CUP (125 ML) FRESH LIME JUICE
- 1/4 TEASPOON GRATED LIME ZEST
- 2 TABLESPOONS GRATED FRESH GINGER
- 1 CLOVE GARLIC, MINCED
- 1 1/2 CUPS (375 ML) EXTRA-VIRGIN OLIVE OIL
- 1 TEASPOON GRANULATED SUGAR
- SALT AND FRESHLY GROUND WHITE PEPPER TO TASTE

In a nonreactive bowl, combine the soy sauce, lime juice, lime zest, ginger and garlic. Slowly whisk in the oil. Season with the sugar, salt and pepper. Cover and refrigerate until ready to use.

green goddess dressing

GREEN GODDESS dressing was created in the 1920s by the chef at San Francisco's Palace Hotel in honor of actor George Arliss who was appearing in a play called "Green Goddess." The classic green goddess dressing is a blend of mayonnaise, tarragon vinegar, parsley, scallions and garlic. In addition to dressing salads, it is often used as a sauce for fish and shellfish.

1 CUP (250 ML) PREPARED OR BASIC MAYONNAISE (PAGE 53)

2 ANCHOVY FILLETS, DRAINED AND FINELY CHOPPED

3 SMALL SCALLIONS, FINELY CHOPPED

1 TABLESPOON FINELY CHOPPED FRESH PARSLEY

1 TABLESPOON TARRAGON VINEGAR

1 TABLESPOON FRESH LEMON JUICE

1 CLOVE GARLIC, CRUSHED

3 TABLESPOONS SOUR CREAM

SALT AND FRESHLY GROUND BLACK PEPPER TO TASTE

In a blender or food processor, purée all the ingredients until smooth. Season to taste with salt and pepper. Transfer to a container. Cover and refrigerate until ready to use.

hazelnut dressing

1/2 CUP (125 ML) ORANGE JUICE

PINCH OF APPLE PIE SPICE

1/2 CUP (125 ML) HAZELNUT OIL

SALT AND FRESHLY GROUND BLACK PEPPER TO TASTE

In a small nonreactive bowl, combine the orange juice and apple pie spice. Slowly whisk in the oil. Season with salt and pepper. Cover and refrigerate until ready to use.

tomato dressing

2 LARGE TOMATOES

2 TEASPOONS TOMATO PASTE

4 TEASPOONS FRESH LEMON JUICE

6 TABLESPOONS EXTRA-VIRGIN OLIVE OIL

SALT AND FRESHLY GROUND BLACK PEPPER TO TASTE

1. In a medium saucepan, bring 1 quart (1 l) of water to a boil. With a paring knife, cut out the stem from the tomato and make a small X in the opposite end. Plunge the tomato in the boiling water and leave it in just until the skin is loosened, 10 to 20 seconds. With a slotted spoon, transfer it to a bowl of cold water to cool. Slip off the skin and cut it in half. Gently but firmly squeeze the seeds from the halves. Dice the tomato.

2. In a blender or food processor, combine the tomato, tomato paste, lemon juice and oil. Purée until smooth. Season with salt and pepper. Transfer to a container. Cover and refrigerate until ready to use.

pastas

WHILE PASTA IS ONE OF OUR MOST FAVORITE FOODS TODAY, it's hardly a new delight. In fact, I know of one English recipe for ravioli that first appeared in the fourteenth century, while variations on macaroni and cheese have been found in cookbooks dating back to the Middle Ages. ⚓ PASTA, IN ALL ITS GUISES, is really no more than a plain cooked paste of wheat flour and water, with or without eggs. The term, however, includes not only the dried semolina and egg noodles of Italy but also the buckwheat, rice and bean thread noodles of Asia, the spaetzle and egg noodles of Europe and the dumplings and stuffed doughs of a wide spectrum of various cuisines and cultures. Pasta is quick, cheap, easy to make and it offers excellent nutritional value. ⚓ PASTA CAN BE SERVED AS AN APPETIZER OR A MAIN COURSE; a good guide is four ounces (120 g) of dry pasta per person for a main course and two to three ounces (60-90 g) for an appetizer. If you're using fresh pasta, double these measurements. ⚓ WHILE FRESH PASTA MIGHT SEEM TO BE THE MOST APPEALING CHOICE, many chefs swear by imported dried Italian pasta. Dried pasta often produces a better texture and bite, and it won't develop a gummy texture. ⚓ PASTA SHOULD ALWAYS BE COOKED IN A LARGE POT OF RAPIDLY BOILING, HEAVILY SALTED WATER. (Ravioli, however, should be cooked at a more gentle boil, to prevent rupturing.) Contrary to popular belief, olive oil does not keep pasta from sticking while cooking. Just make sure you have enough water and keep it at a steady, heavy boil and stir the pot often. If you lose your boil after adding the pasta, simply cover the pot, bring back to the boil and then remove the cover. After draining the pasta thoroughly, add a tablespoon or two of high-quality olive oil. ⚓ THE SIZE AND SHAPE OF THE NOODLE YOU CHOOSE IS TOTALLY UP TO YOU, but pick your pasta with your other ingredients and sauce in mind. When I make pasta, I always prepare extra, so we can eat it cold (or reheated) the next day. The recipes that follow are so good, however, you're unlikely to have leftovers at all.

VOYAGER OF THE SEAS

linguine bolognese

NAMED AFTER THE RICH COOKERY STYLE OF BOLOGNA, Italy, Bolognese refers to dishes served with a thick, full-bodied meat and vegetable sauce enhanced with wine and milk or cream. Linguini is the most popular type of pasta to use for this dish. In Italian, it means "little tongues." It is long, narrow and flat. Sometimes it is referred to as flat spaghetti.

2 TABLESPOONS EXTRA-VIRGIN OLIVE OIL

1/2 POUND (225 G) GROUND BEEF

3 SLICES BACON, FINELY DICED

1 MEDIUM ONION, FINELY DICED

4 CLOVES GARLIC, MINCED

2 MEDIUM CARROTS, FINELY DICED

1 STALK CELERY, FINELY DICED

3 RIPE MEDIUM TOMATOES OR 1 16-OUNCE (480 G) CAN WHOLE ITALIAN-STYLE TOMATOES

1/2 TABLESPOON CHOPPED FRESH THYME LEAVES

1/2 TABLESPOON CHOPPED FRESH OREGANO LEAVES

1 TABLESPOON CHOPPED FRESH BASIL LEAVES

2 CUPS (500 ML) DRY RED WINE

1 BAY LEAF

3 TABLESPOONS CANNED TOMATO PURÉE

1 TABLESPOON GRANULATED SUGAR

SALT AND FRESHLY GROUND BLACK PEPPER TO TASTE

1 POUND (454 G) DRIED LINGUINE

1 CUP (140 G) SHAVED PARMESAN CHEESE, SUCH AS PARMIGIANO-REGGIANO

FRESH BASIL LEAVES FOR GARNISH

1. In a large skillet, heat the oil over medium heat. Add the ground beef and bacon and cook, stirring, until browned. Add the onion, garlic, carrots and celery. Cook, stirring, until the vegetables soften.

2. Meanwhile, in a medium saucepan, bring 1 quart (1 l) water to a boil. With a paring knife, cut out the stems from the tomatoes and make a small X in the opposite ends. Plunge the tomatoes in the boiling water and leave them in just until the skins are loosened, 10 to 20 seconds. With a slotted spoon, transfer the tomatoes to a bowl of cold water to cool. Slip off the skins and cut the tomatoes in half. Gently but firmly squeeze the seeds from the halves. Dice the tomatoes.

3. Add the herbs, wine and bay leaf. Cook until the wine is reduced by half. Stir in the tomato purée, chopped tomatoes and sugar. Season with salt and pepper. Bring to a simmer and cook on low heat, stirring occasionally, until thickened, about 40 to 60 minutes.

4. Cook the linguine in a stockpot of boiling salted water until *al dente*, 6 to 8 minutes. Drain the pasta and return it to the pot. Add two-thirds of the sauce and toss to coat. To serve, transfer the pasta to a large warmed serving bowl and top with the remaining sauce. Garnish with the Parmesan and basil leaves and serve immediately

Note: If using canned tomatoes, simply remove them from the liquid and dice.

rigatoni pesto

pastas

PESTO IS AN UNCOOKED SAUCE made with fresh basil, garlic, pine nuts, Parmesan or Pecorino Romano cheese and olive oil. This classic, fresh tasting sauce originated in Genoa, Italy, and although used in a variety of dishes, it is a favorite with pasta.

1 CUP (140 G) PINE NUTS

2 CUPS (280 G) FRESH BASIL LEAVES

4 MEDIUM CLOVES GARLIC

1 CUP (250 ML) EXTRA-VIRGIN OLIVE OIL

1¼ CUPS (175 G) GRATED PARMESAN CHEESE

SALT AND FRESHLY GROUND BLACK PEPPER TO TASTE

1 POUND (454 G) DRIED RIGATONI

2 CUPS (500 ML) HEAVY CREAM

CHOPPED FRESH BASIL FOR GARNISH

1. In a dry skillet over high heat, toss or stir the pine nuts, taking care not to scorch them, until lightly browned. Transfer them to a small bowl and let cool.

2. In a food processor, combine the basil leaves, garlic and pine nuts. Process until finely chopped. With the motor running, slowly add the oil through the feed tube, stopping once or twice to scrape down the sides. Add 1 cup (140 g) of the Parmesan cheese and season with salt and pepper. Process briefly until combined. Transfer to a bowl, cover and set aside.

3. Cook the rigatoni in a stockpot of boiling salted water until *al dente*, 6 to 8 minutes. Meanwhile, in a large saucepan, bring the cream to a boil over low to medium heat. Be careful not to scorch the cream. Reduce the heat and simmer, stirring occasionally, until the cream is reduced by half. Remove from the heat and stir in the pesto.

4. To serve, drain the pasta and add it to the sauce. Toss to coat. Transfer the pasta to a large warmed serving bowl. Garnish with chopped basil and remaining Parmesan cheese. Serve immediately.

Note: Serve with extra pesto sauce on the side. It is great for spreading on bread.

linguine del giorno

YIELD: 4 TO 6 SERVINGS

1 CUP (250 ML) DRY WHITE WINE

2 DOZEN LITTLENECK CLAMS, SCRUBBED WELL UNDER COLD WATER

2 POUNDS (905 G) RIPE TOMATOES

3 TABLESPOONS EXTRA-VIRGIN OLIVE OIL

1⅓ CUPS (190 G) FINELY DICED PANCETTA

2 MEDIUM SHALLOTS, MINCED

1 MEDIUM LEEK, WHITE PART ONLY, WASHED AND CUT INTO JULIENNE STRIPS

6 CLOVES GARLIC, MINCED

3 TABLESPOONS CHOPPED FRESH ITALIAN PARSLEY

½ TEASPOON CRUSHED RED PEPPER

SALT AND FRESHLY GROUND BLACK PEPPER TO TASTE

1 POUND (454 G) DRIED LINGUINE

GRATED PARMESAN CHEESE FOR GARNISH

1. In a large stockpot, heat the wine over medium heat. Add the clams. Cover and steam for 3 to 4 minutes, shaking the pot occasionally. Begin checking the clams; as they open, transfer them to a colander placed over a bowl. Discard any clams that do not open.

2. Strain the clam broth—from both the cooking pot and the bowl—through a fine sieve lined with cheesecloth into a small bowl. Set aside. Remove the shells from the clams. Set the clams aside.

3. In a large saucepan, bring 2 quarts (2 l) of water to a boil. Meanwhile, with a paring knife, cut out the stems from the tomatoes and make a small X in the opposite ends. Working in batches, plunge the tomatoes in the boiling water and leave them in just until the skins are loosened, 10 to 20 seconds. With a slotted spoon, transfer the tomatoes to a large bowl of cold water to cool. Slip off the skins and cut the tomatoes in half. Gently but firmly squeeze the seeds from the halves. Dice the tomatoes and reserve.

4. In a large skillet, heat the oil over medium heat. Add the pancetta and cook, stirring, until browned. Add the shallots, leek and garlic, and sauté until the shallots soften and become translucent.

5. Add the reserved clam broth, parsley and crushed red pepper. Bring to a boil. Reduce the heat and simmer, stirring, for 5 minutes. Add the reserved clams and diced tomatoes. Season with salt and pepper. Transfer the sauce to a large warmed serving bowl and keep warm.

6. Meanwhile, cook the linguine in a stockpot of boiling salted water until *al dente*, 6 to 8 minutes. To serve, drain the pasta and add it to the sauce. Toss to coat. Garnish with chopped parsley and grated Parmesan and serve immediately.

spaghetti carbonara

CARBONARA IS THE ITALIAN TERM DESCRIBING A PASTA DISH OF SPAGHETTI (or other noodles) with a sauce traditionally composed of cream, eggs, Parmesan cheese and bacon. In this case pancetta is being used instead of bacon and eggs are not used. A great addition to this dish is peas, which add both flavor and color.

3 CUPS (750 ML) HEAVY CREAM

1 TABLESPOON EXTRA-VIRGIN OLIVE OIL

1 POUND (454 G) PANCETTA, DICED

1 POUND (454 G) DRIED SPAGHETTI

SALT AND FRESHLY GROUND BLACK PEPPER TO TASTE

1/3 CUP (50 G) CHOPPED FRESH ITALIAN PARSLEY

GRATED PARMESAN CHEESE FOR GARNISH

1. In a large heavy saucepan, bring the cream to a boil. Reduce the heat to low and simmer, uncovered, until the cream is reduced by half. Be sure not to scorch the cream. Remove the pan from the heat.

2. In a large skillet, heat the oil over medium heat. Add the pancetta and cook, stirring, until crisp. With a slotted spoon, transfer the pancetta to a plate lined with paper towels to drain.

3. Cook the spaghetti in a stockpot of boiling salted water until *al dente*, 6 to 8 minutes. To serve, drain the pasta and add it to the cream. Toss to coat. Season with salt and pepper. Transfer to a large warmed serving bowl and sprinkle with the pancetta. Garnish with the parsley and Parmesan and serve immediately.

seafood fettuccine

1 CUP (250 ML) DRY WHITE WINE

2 DOZEN MUSSELS, DEBEARDED
AND SCRUBBED WELL UNDER
COLD WATER

3 TABLESPOONS EXTRA-VIRGIN
OLIVE OIL

1 MEDIUM ONION, FINELY DICED

6 CLOVES GARLIC, MINCED

1/2 POUND (225 G) MEDIUM
SHRIMP, PEELED AND DEVEINED

1/2 POUND (225 G) SEA
SCALLOPS, CLEANED

3 TABLESPOONS CHOPPED
FRESH BASIL

3 TABLESPOONS CHOPPED
FRESH ITALIAN PARSLEY

1/2 TEASPOON CRUSHED
RED PEPPER

1 TABLESPOON PERNOD

2 POUNDS (905 G) RIPE
TOMATOES, PEELED,
SEEDED AND DICED

1/8 TEASPOON SALT

1/8 TEASPOON FRESHLY GROUND
BLACK PEPPER

1 POUND (454 G) DRIED
FETTUCCINE

CHOPPED FRESH ITALIAN
PARSLEY FOR GARNISH

1. In a large stockpot, heat the wine over medium heat. Add the mussels. Cover and steam for 2 minutes, shaking the pot occasionally. Begin checking the mussels; as they open, transfer them to a colander placed over a bowl. Total steaming time will be about 4 minutes. Discard any mussels that do not open.

2. Strain the mussel broth—from both the cooking pot and the bowl—through a fine sieve lined with cheesecloth into a small bowl. Set aside. Remove the shells from the mussels. Set the mussels aside.

3. In a large saucepan, bring 2 quarts (2 l) of water to a boil. Meanwhile, with a paring knife, cut out the stems from the tomatoes and make a small X in the opposite ends. Working in batches, plunge the tomatoes in the boiling water and leave them in just until the skins are loosened, 10 to 20 seconds. With a slotted spoon, transfer the tomatoes to a large bowl of cold water to cool. Slip off the skins and cut the tomatoes in half. Gently but firmly squeeze the seeds from the halves. Dice the tomatoes and reserve.

4. In a large skillet, heat the oil over medium heat. Add the onion and garlic and cook, stirring, until softened and translucent. Add the shrimp and scallops and cook until just opaque. Stir in the basil, parsley and crushed red pepper.

5. Add the reserved mussel broth and Pernod. Bring to a boil. Reduce the heat and simmer, stirring, for 5 minutes. Add the reserved mussels and diced tomatoes. Season with salt and pepper. Bring to a simmer. Immediately transfer the sauce to a large warmed serving bowl and keep warm.

6. Meanwhile, cook the fettuccine in a stockpot of boiling salted water until *al dente*, 6 to 8 minutes. To serve, drain the pasta and add it to the sauce. Toss to coat. Garnish with chopped parsley and serve immediately.

ziti santa fe

pastas

Roasted Garlic Pesto

1 HEAD GARLIC

SALT AND FRESHLY GROUND BLACK PEPPER
TO TASTE

1 CUP (140 G) PINE NUTS

2 CUPS (280 G) FRESH BASIL LEAVES

1 CUP (250 ML) EXTRA-VIRGIN OLIVE OIL

1 1/4 CUPS (175 G) GRATED PARMESAN CHEESE

1. To roast the garlic, preheat the oven to
325°F/160°C. Pull the papery husk off the
garlic head. Slice the tip off the head to expose
the cloves. Rub with some oil and season with
salt and pepper. Place in an ovenproof dish,
sprinkle with a bit of water, and cover with
aluminum foil. Roast for 40 to 45 minutes, or
until very tender. Let cool. Squeeze the garlic
pulp from the skins into a bowl and reserve.

2. Meanwhile, toast the pine nuts: In a dry skillet
over high heat, toss or stir the pine nuts, taking
care not to scorch them, until lightly browned.
Transfer them to a small bowl and let cool.

3. In a food processor, combine the basil leaves,
pine nuts and 2 tablespoons roasted garlic (save
the remaining garlic for another use). Process
until finely chopped. With the motor running,
slowly add the oil through the feed tube, stopping
once or twice to scrape down the sides. Add the
Parmesan and season with salt and pepper. Process
briefly until combined. Transfer to a bowl, cover,
and set aside.

To Assemble

3 TABLESPOONS EXTRA-VIRGIN OLIVE OIL

2 MEDIUM SHALLOTS, FINELY DICED

1 POUND (454 G) PORTOBELLO MUSHROOMS,
WIPED CLEAN AND SLICED

1/2 CUP (125 ML) DRY WHITE WINE

1/4 POUND (112 G) SMOKED TURKEY,
CUT INTO JULIENNE STRIPS

1 CUP (140 G) DICED RED PIMIENTO

1/2 CUP (125 ML) ROASTED GARLIC PESTO

SALT AND FRESHLY GROUND BLACK PEPPER
TO TASTE

1 POUND (454 G) DRIED ZITI

SHAVED PARMESAN CHEESE FOR GARNISH

WHOLE FRESH SAGE LEAVES FOR GARNISH

1. In a large sauté pan, heat the oil over medium-
high heat. Add the shallots and mushrooms and
cook, stirring, for 5 minutes. Add the wine and
simmer until the liquid is reduced by half. Add
the smoked turkey and pimiento and cook until
heated through.

2. Take off the heat and add the roasted pesto
and toss until well combined. Season with salt
and pepper. Transfer the sauce to a large warmed
serving bowl and keep warm.

3. Meanwhile, cook the ziti in a stockpot of
boiling salted water until *al dente*, 6 to 8
minutes. To serve, drain the pasta and add it
to the sauce. Toss to coat. Garnish with shaved
Parmesan and sage leaves and serve immediately.

Note: Although this recipe calls for smoked
turkey, regular turkey will work just as well.

entrées

FOR COOKS EVERYWHERE, the entrée is the *piece de resistance*, the main event on which the rest of the meal is based. It's almost always the most expensive and time-consuming part of the meal to prepare, and you want it be perfect. ⚓ WITH THAT IN MIND, you'll find recipes here for wonderful entrées that work each and every time. These are dishes that turn out perfectly whether we're cooking them for hundreds on board a ship, or I'm making them for my family of five at home.

Beef WHEN YOU DECIDE TO SPLURGE, find the best beef you can buy: prime or choice grade. The more the meat is marbled with fat, the more tender the steak will be.

Poultry AT THE TURN OF THE CENTURY and for a long time afterward, chicken was considered an expensive treat, to be served mainly for special occasions. Today, chicken is cheap, and great for weight-watchers as well. All poultry—and game birds—offer excellent nutritional value. Not only are they sources of complete protein, they're rich in calcium, iron and phosphorus. Chicken is compatible with so many seasonings, sauces and preparation techniques that there's no excuse whatsoever to turn out a boring bird.

Veal MANY OF THE RECIPES for veal that we enjoy today had their origin in the kitchens of the great chefs of France and Italy. ⚓ VEAL refers to the flesh of a young calf, between one and 26 weeks old. Conventional veal, older calves up to 26 weeks, drink their mothers' milk at birth but are weaned at 24 hours. Most veal sold in American supermarkets is conventional veal. ⚓ THE HIGHEST-QUALITY VEAL in the market is nature veal, which comes from calves that drink only milk or milk replacements before they come to market at 16 or 17 weeks old. ⚓ ALL EUROPEAN VEAL is nature veal, which is why so many people come back from vacation raving about the veal dishes they've eaten. But in the United States, you will have to go to the best butcher shops or specialty markets to find nature veal, and you'll pay a higher price.

MONARCH OF THE SEAS

Pork PORK IS OUR MOST VERSATILE MEAT, and provides a wealth of flavor. Pork that has been raised and handled properly can rival veal and lamb for tenderness and delicacy of flavor. ⚓ WHEN BUYING PORK, look for firm, white fat with fresh red bones under the fat. ⚓ PORK CHOPS AND STEAKS WILL BE MORE TENDER, juicy and flavorful if cooked at a lower temperature. High grill or broiler temperatures overcook the outside before the inside reaches the desired degree of doneness. An absolute essential for success in roasting any meat, particularly pork, is a good meat thermometer.

Lamb TO QUALIFY AS LAMB in the American marketplace, the animal can be no more than 12 months of age; the average is half of that. Most lamb reaches market at six months or younger. At that age, it's all tender. It hasn't lived long enough to get tough. ⚓ LAMB WILL KEEP FOR UP TO A WEEK in the refrigerator. It can be prepared ahead of time for cooking and can be frozen in the same manner as pork. ⚓ Spring lamb is the best, but it's available for only a short time. The flavor is very mild, and the meat is juicier and more tender. ⚓ TODAY you can also find high-quality frozen lamb in many markets. Look for light-weight cuts, because younger lamb will be more tender and flavorful.

Fish FISH OFFERS A GREATER VARIETY of textures and flavors than any other animal protein. It also has less fat—a boon in these cholesterol-conscious times. ⚓ Buy the highest-quality fish you can find, from a store you trust. Fish is not subject to the inspections and regulations that meat is, so the range in quality can be huge. Always shop at a store where they do a brisk business (this means high turnover and fresher fish) and one where the staff is knowledgeable and willing to answer your questions. ⚓ IF YOU'RE BUYING FILLETS OR STEAKS, they should be neatly cut into the appropriate thickness for cooking. Use the same criteria for fresh-ness as you would a whole fish—color, smell and touch. ⚓ Whatever you do, don't overcook it. Fish has a delicate texture and flavor, which can be easily ruined by overcooking. Remove it from heat while it remains translucent in the very center because it will continue to cook in its own heat. ⚓ IF YOU'RE USING FROZEN FISH, defrost it in the refrigerator for 24 to 36 hours to preserve its texture. Otherwise, you'll get soggy fish. For all entrées, Royal Culinary Collections spice mixes will enhance the flavor of your dishes.

roasted filet mignon
with brandy-peppercorn sauce

entrées

FILET MIGNON, also called the tenderloin, is one of the most popular cuts of meat available. It is a boneless cut of beef that comes from the small end of the tenderloin. It is usually 1 to 2 inches (2.5-5 cm) thick and 1 1/2 to 3 inches (3.75-7.5 cm) in diameter. This cut of meat is extremely tender and goes well with any sauce paired with it. I definitely suggest serving it with the creamy peppercorn sauce. The spiciness of the peppercorn sauce will be mellowed by the taste of the filet.

4 5-OUNCE (142 G) FILET MIGNON STEAKS

1/4 TEASPOON BLACK PEPPERCORNS, CRUSHED

1/4 TEASPOON WHITE PEPPERCORNS, CRUSHED

2 TABLESPOONS EXTRA-VIRGIN OLIVE OIL

2 TABLESPOONS FINELY CHOPPED SHALLOT

1/4 POUND (112 G) MIXED FRESH MUSHROOMS (SUCH AS WHITE BUTTON, CREMINI AND PORCINI), SLICED

2 TABLESPOONS BALSAMIC VINEGAR

1 1/2 CUPS (375 ML) BEEF STOCK (SEE PAGE 151)

1/4 CUP (60 ML) BRANDY

1 TABLESPOON CHOPPED FRESH THYME

1/2 CUP (125 ML) CANNED HEAVY CREAM

1 TEASPOON CORNSTARCH MIXED WITH 1 TABLESPOON WATER

1 TABLESPOON GREEN PEPPERCORNS, CANNED

SALT TO TASTE

1/2 CUP (70 G) HARICOT VERTS (THIN GREEN BEANS) AND RED PEPPER STRIPS AS A GARNISH

2 TABLESPOONS UNSALTED BUTTER

1. Preheat the oven to 450°F/230°C. Roll the filets in the crushed black and white peppercorns. In a large heavy ovenproof skillet or cast-iron pan, heat 1 tablespoon oil over medium-high heat. Add the filets and sear them on both sides until golden brown, 8 minutes on each side. Transfer the skillet to the oven and roast for 7 to 8 minutes, turning the filets once after 3 to 4 minutes.

2. Meanwhile, in a nonreactive saucepan, heat the remaining 1 tablespoon oil over medium-high heat. Add the shallot and cook, stirring, until golden brown, about 5 minutes. Add the mushrooms and vinegar and sauté until most of the liquid is evaporated. Add the beef stock, brandy and thyme. Simmer until the liquid is reduced by half.

3. Add the heavy cream. Just before the mixture comes to a boil, whisk in the cornstarch mixture. Season with salt and stir in the green peppercorns.

4. While the sauce and meat are both cooking prepare the vegetables. In a pot of boiling salted water, add the haricots verts and cook for 2 minutes or until they turn bright green. Immediately remove and place in a bowl of ice water. Remove them and set aside once they are cold. Meanwhile in a sauté pan, melt 2 tablespoons of butter, add the red pepper strips and haricots verts. Toss to coat with the butter, season with salt and pepper and remove from the pan.

5. To serve, divide the filets among warmed plates. Spoon 3 or 4 tablespoons of sauce over each filet and garnish with haricots verts and red pepper strips. Serve immediately.

Note: Canned green peppercorns are packed in brine and are available canned or in jars.

grilled beef
with chimichurri sauce

entrées

YIELD: 6 SERVINGS

CHIMICHURRI SAUCE is as common in Argentina as ketchup is in the United States. This thick herb sauce is a melange of olive oil, chopped parsley, oregano, onion and garlic, all seasoned with salt, cayenne, and crushed red and black pepper. In Argentina, It is a must with grilled meat and a common accompaniment to a variety of other dishes. As an alternative, you can use the Royal Culinary Collections™ Steak Sauce.

1 CUP (250 ML) EXTRA-VIRGIN OLIVE OIL

1/4 CUP (60 ML) CHAMPAGNE VINEGAR

1/4 CUP (60 ML) FRESH LIME JUICE

1/4 CUP (35 G) CHOPPED FRESH OREGANO

1/4 CUP (35 G) CHOPPED FRESH PARSLEY

3 CLOVES GARLIC, FINELY CHOPPED

1 TEASPOON CRUSHED RED PEPPER

1/2 TEASPOON CAYENNE PEPPER

SALT AND FRESHLY GROUND BLACK PEPPER TO TASTE

2 1/4 POUNDS (1 KG) TENDERLOIN (BEEF FILLET) OR STRIP LOIN STEAK, TRIMMED OF FAT AND TIED WITH TWINE (SEE NOTE, BELOW)

APPLE OR PECAN WOOD CHIPS

1. Make the chimichurri sauce: In a nonreactive bowl, combine the oil, vinegar, lime juice, oregano, parsley, garlic and crushed red pepper. Season with salt, pepper and cayenne.

2. Place the beef in a zipper-lock plastic bag and add 3/4 cup (200 ml) chimichurri sauce. Remove excess air from the bag, seal it and squeeze the bag to coat the beef with the sauce. Let marinate in the refrigerator for 2 hours. Cover the remaining sauce and refrigerate.

3. About 30 minutes before grilling, remove the beef and reserved sauce from the refrigerator and soak the wood chips in cold water. Heat a covered charcoal or gas grill to medium hot. Just before cooking, toss the wood chips onto the hot coals or add them to the gas grill according to the manufacturer's instructions.

4. Grill the beef, turning occasionally and basting with the marinade from the bag until the outside is well browned and the inside is cooked to the desired doneness, about 10 to 20 minutes per pound. (An instant-read thermometer should register 125°F/52°C for medium-rare or 135°F/57°C for medium.) Discard any remaining marinade from the bag.

5. Transfer the beef to a cutting board and let rest for 10 minutes. Slice and transfer to a warmed serving platter. Drizzle the slices with some of the reserved chimichurri sauce and serve.

Note: If using a strip loin, leave a 1/2-inch (1.25 cm) layer of fat around the roast. For individual steaks, cut the meat into 6-ounce (170 g) portions, about 1 1/2 inches (3.75 cm) thick. Sear in a hot pan for 2 minutes on each side and then grill for 4 to 5 minutes on each side to the desired doneness.

grilled island strip steak
with caramelized onion
and rum glaze

STRIP STEAK, also known as New York strip steak or shell steak, is a cut that comes from the short loin. It is the boneless top loin muscle and is equivalent to a Porterhouse without the tenderloin and bone. Depending on the region, it may also be marketed as Delmonico, Kansas City strip or Sirloin club steak. Although it can be prepared in a number of different ways, grilling brings out the best flavor of this cut of meat.

The process for producing molasses is an interesting one. During the refining of sugar cane and sugar beets, the juice squeezed from these plants is boiled to a syrupy mixture from which sugar crystals are extracted. There are three types of molasses that are used today. Light molasses comes from the first boiling of the sugar syrup and is lightest in both flavor and color. Dark molasses, which comes from a second boiling, is darker, thicker and less sweet. Blackstrap comes from the third boiling and is the darkest of the three. For this dish, I would recommend using the dark molasses. Its flavor will pair well with the onions and steak.

2 TABLESPOONS UNSALTED BUTTER

2 MEDIUM SHALLOTS, MINCED

1 SMALL ONION, CUT IN HALF FROM POLE TO POLE AND THINLY SLICED

3 CLOVES GARLIC, MINCED

1 CUP (250 ML) DARK RUM

3 CUPS (750 ML) BEEF STOCK (SEE PAGE 151)

2 TABLESPOONS MOLASSES

4 8-OUNCE (226 G) STRIP LOIN STEAKS

SALT AND FRESHLY GROUND BLACK PEPPER TO TASTE

1. In a saucepan, heat the butter over medium-high heat. Add the shallots, onion and garlic. Cook, stirring, until softened and translucent, about 5 minutes. Add the rum and simmer until the liquid is reduced to $1/3$ (75 ml) cup. Add the beef stock and bring to a boil. Reduce the heat and whisk in the molasses. Simmer until the liquid is reduced to 2 cups (500 ml).

2. Heat a charcoal or gas grill. Season the steaks with salt and pepper. Grill on both sides to the desired doneness. To serve, place the strip steaks on warmed plates and top with the caramelized onion and its glaze. Serve immediately.

Note: You can enhance the flavor of this dish with our delicate Tropical Banana Rum Hot Sauce from the Royal Culinary Collections™.

osso buco
with risotto

entrées

Osso Buco is an Italian dish made of veal shanks braised in olive oil, white wine, stock, onions, tomatoes, garlic, carrots, celery and fresh herbs. Traditionally it is served with risotto and garnished with *gremolata* (made of minced parsley and lemon peel). *Gremolata* gives the dish a fresh, sprightly flavor.

Risotto is an Italian rice specialty made by stirring hot stock into a mixture of rice (and often chopped onions) that has been sautéed in butter. The stock is added a little at a time and the mixture is stirred continually while it cooks until all the liquid has absorbed before more stock is added. This technique results in rice that is delectably creamy while the grains remain separate and firm.

Veal Shanks

3 TABLESPOONS UNSALTED BUTTER

6 VEAL SHANKS

1/2 TEASPOON SALT

1 TEASPOON FRESHLY GROUND BLACK PEPPER

1/2 TEASPOON CHOPPED FRESH THYME

1/2 TEASPOON CHOPPED FRESH MARJORAM

2 BAY LEAVES, CRUSHED

1 CUP (140 G) CHOPPED ONION

1/2 CUP (70 G) CHOPPED CARROT

1/2 CUP (70 G) CHOPPED CELERY

2 CUPS (500 ML) DRY WHITE WINE

6 CLOVES GARLIC, CRUSHED

1 1/4 POUNDS (566 G) RIPE TOMATOES, DICED

2 TABLESPOONS TOMATO PASTE

ROSEMARY SPRIGS AS GARNISH

1. Clarify the butter: Melt the butter in a small saucepan over low heat. Cook until the butterfat becomes clear and the milk solids drop to the bottom of the pan. Skim the surface foam as the butter separates. Carefully spoon the clear butterfat into a small bowl. Discard the milky liquid at the bottom of the saucepan.

2. Preheat the oven to 315°F/160°C. Rub the shanks with the salt, pepper, thyme, marjoram and bay leaves. In a large heavy skillet, heat the clarified butter over medium-high heat. Add the shanks, in batches, and sauté until gently browned on all sides. With a pair of tongs, transfer the shanks as each is browned to a large flameproof casserole or Dutch oven.

3. Add the onion, carrot and celery to the skillet and cook, stirring, over medium heat until golden. Transfer the vegetables to the casserole. Add the wine, garlic, tomatoes and tomato paste to the skillet. Scrape up any browned bits from the bottom of the pan and transfer the contents of the skillet to the casserole.

4. Bake the shanks, uncovered, for 1 1/2 hours, basting with the pan juices every 5 minutes, until the meat is tender. With a pair of tongs, transfer the shanks to a warmed platter.

5. Strain the sauce through a fine sieve into a saucepan and discard the vegetables left behind. Bring the sauce to a simmer over medium heat and skim the fat from the surface. Cook, stirring, until the sauce lightly coats the back of a spoon. (If the sauce is too thin, add 1 teaspoon flour mixed with 1 tablespoon butter and cook, stirring, until thickened.) Adjust the seasonings and keep warm over very low heat.

Risotto

3 TABLESPOONS UNSALTED BUTTER

1 MEDIUM ONION, FINELY CHOPPED

1 CUP (140 G) ARBORIO RICE

3 CUPS (750 ML) BEEF OR CHICKEN STOCK (SEE PAGE 151 OR 152)

SALT AND FRESHLY GROUND WHITE PEPPER TO TASTE

2 TABLESPOONS GRATED PARMESAN CHEESE

1. In a heavy saucepan or flameproof casserole, heat the butter over medium heat. Add the onion and cook, stirring, until softened, about 2 minutes. Add the rice and stir with a wooden spoon until a toasted aroma develops, about 4 minutes.

2. Reduce the heat to low, and add the stock $1/3$ at a time, stirring constantly. Continue to cook until the rice is tender and the liquid is absorbed, about 15 minutes. Season with salt and pepper and sprinkle with the cheese. Keep warm until ready to serve.

Gremolata

4 TABLESPOONS CHOPPED FRESH ITALIAN PARSLEY

2 TABLESPOONS CHOPPED FRESH CURLY PARSLEY

2 TABLESPOONS GRATED LEMON ZEST

Bring to a simmer over medium heat. In a small bowl, combine both types of chopped parsley and lemon zest.

To serve this dish, place the risotto on the plate, top with a veal shank, sprinkle with *gremolata* and garnish with a sprig of rosemary.

Note: A secret tip regarding rosemary. Heat about 2 inches (5 cm) of vegetable oil in a frying pan. Once hot (to test: place a piece of bread in oil to make sure; if it browns the oil is ready) place the rosemary in for about 20 seconds. Quickly remove once it turns bright green and drain on paper towels. Sprinkle powdered sugar on top of the rosemary. *Voila*—the taste and aroma are outstanding!

pan-seared veal chops
with brandy-mustard sauce

2 TABLESPOONS EXTRA-VIRGIN
OLIVE OIL

4 14-OUNCE (396 G) VEAL CHOPS

SALT AND FRESHLY GROUND
BLACK PEPPER TO TASTE

2 MEDIUM SHALLOTS, MINCED

1 CUP (140 G) CHOPPED
MIXED FRESH MUSHROOMS
(SUCH AS OYSTER, CREMINI
AND SHIITAKE)

3/4 CUP (200 ML) BEEF
OR CHICKEN STOCK
(SEE PAGE 151 OR 152)

1/4 CUP (60 ML) BRANDY

1 TABLESPOON TOMATO PASTE

1 TABLESPOON CHOPPED FRESH
TARRAGON

1 TABLESPOON TARRAGON
MUSTARD

1. Preheat the oven to 400°F/200°C. In a sauté pan, heat the oil over medium-high heat. Season the veal chops with salt and pepper and add to the pan. Sear on both sides until golden brown but still undercooked. Transfer to a baking sheet and bake for 15 minutes, or to the desired doneness.

2. While the chops are baking, add the shallots and mushrooms to the sauté pan. Cook, stirring, until the shallots become softened and translucent. Add the stock, brandy, tomato paste and tarragon. Scrape up any browned bits from the bottom of the pan and stir to dissolve them. Simmer, stirring occasionally, until the liquid is reduced by half.

3. Stir in the mustard and immediately remove the pan from the heat. To serve, divide the veal chops among 4 warmed plates and surround with the sauce. Serve immediately.

Note: Canned chicken broth or water will work just as well if you do not have any stock on hand.

veal cordon bleu
with mushroom sauce and glazed carrots

entrées

YIELD: 4 SERVINGS

2 POUNDS (905 G) VEAL
TOP ROUND, SLICED INTO
5-TO-6-OUNCE (142-170 G)
CUTLETS

6 THIN SLICES HAM

6 THIN SLICES GRUYÈRE CHEESE

1/2 CUP (70 G) ALL-PURPOSE
FLOUR

2 LARGE EGGS, BEATEN WITH
1 TABLESPOON WHOLE MILK

1 CUP (140 G) FRESH BREAD
CRUMBS

SALT AND FRESHLY GROUND
BLACK PEPPER TO TASTE

1 TABLESPOON UNSALTED BUTTER

1/4 CUP (35 G) MINCED SHALLOT

8 SMALL WHITE MUSHROOMS,
WIPED CLEAN AND SLICED

1/4 CUP (60 ML) DRY WHITE WINE

1 1/2 CUPS (375 ML) BROWN
SAUCE (SEE PAGE 149)

1/4 CUP (60 ML) HEAVY CREAM

1/2 TABLESPOON CHOPPED FRESH
PARSLEY

4 TABLESPOONS CANOLA OIL,
PLUS EXTRA AS NEEDED

1/2 POUND (225 G) CARROTS
PEELED AND CUT ON THE
DIAGONAL

1 TABLESPOON BUTTER,
UNSALTED

1 TABLESPOON ORANGE
JUICE

1 TABLESPOON BROWN SUGAR

CHOPPED PARSLEY
FOR GARNISH

1. Make the veal rolls: Place a veal cutlet on a cutting board. With the side of a meat mallet, flatten the cutlet evenly to enlarge its circumference. Repeat with the remaining cutlets. Place a slice of ham on a plate. Top with a slice of cheese and roll into cylinder. Repeat with the remaining ham and cheese. Center a ham roll onto each veal cutlet and fold the meat around it. Cover with plastic wrap and refrigerate until firm.

2. Place the flour, eggs and bread crumbs in separate shallow dishes. Season each lightly with salt and pepper. Dredge each veal roll in flour and shake off the excess. Dip quickly in the eggs and then roll in the breadcrumbs. Transfer the rolls to a plate, cover with plastic wrap and refrigerate for 30 to 60 minutes.

3. Meanwhile, make the mushroom sauce. In a sauté pan, heat the butter over medium heat. Add the shallot and cook, stirring, until softened and translucent. Add the mushrooms and sauté until slightly browned. Add the wine and cook, stirring, until reduced by half. Add the brown sauce and simmer, stirring, for 15 to 20 minutes.

Stir in the heavy cream and parsley. Season with salt and pepper and keep warm over very low heat.

4. Preheat the oven to 350°F/180°C. Lightly coat a baking sheet with vegetable oil spray. In a skillet, heat half the oil over medium-high heat. Add half the veal rolls and sauté until golden all the way around, about 10 minutes. Transfer to the prepared baking sheet. Repeat with the remaining oil and rolls. Bake the veal rolls for 20 minutes, or until cooked through but not dry.

5. For the carrots, add them to a 1 quart (1 l) pot of boiling salted water. Cook them for 8 to 10 minutes. Drain in a colander. In a small sauté pan, add the butter, orange juice and sugar. Cook over low heat for one minute. Add the carrots and toss. Cook for about 5 minutes until they have a shiny glaze.

6. To serve, transfer the veal rolls to a clean cutting board and slice each into 2 diagonal slices. Serve with glazed carrots sprinkled with chopped parsley and sauce on the side. Serve immediately.

grandmother's sunday roast chicken

1 4-POUND (1.8 KG) ROASTING CHICKEN

4 TABLESPOONS UNSALTED BUTTER, SOFTENED

1³/₄ CUPS (240 G) CHOPPED ONION

4 TEASPOONS MINCED GARLIC

GIBLETS FROM THE CHICKEN, CHOPPED

1 TABLESPOON CHOPPED FRESH THYME LEAVES

1 TABLESPOON CHOPPED FRESH MARJORAM OR BASIL LEAVES

¹/₂ CUP (70 G) CHOPPED FRESH ITALIAN PARSLEY

1 BAY LEAF, CRUSHED

2 CUPS (280 G) STORE-BOUGHT BREAD CRUMBS

SALT AND FRESHLY GROUND BLACK PEPPER TO TASTE

³/₄ CUP (100 G) CHOPPED CARROT

¹/₄ CUP (35 G) CHOPPED CELERY

1 TABLESPOON ALL-PURPOSE FLOUR

²/₃ CUP (150 ML) DRY WHITE WINE

1 TABLESPOON RED WINE VINEGAR

1¹/₄ CUPS (310 ML) WATER OR CHICKEN STOCK (SEE PAGE 152)

1. Preheat the oven to 350°F/175°C. Rinse the chicken inside and out with cold water and pat dry with paper towels. Set aside.

2. In a large skillet, heat 2 tablespoons butter over medium heat. Add 1¹/₄ cups (175 g) onion, ¹/₄ cup (35 g) carrots, ¹/₄ cup (35 g) celery and 3 teaspoons garlic and cook until the onion is softened and becomes translucent. Add the giblets and cook just until browned.

3. Add the thyme, marjoram or basil, parsley and bay leaf. Stir until fragrant. Stir in the bread-crumbs and season with salt and pepper. Remove from the heat and let cool completely.

4. Season the cavity of the chicken with salt and pepper. Spoon the stuffing into the chicken and place a teaspoon of stuffing between the skin and each breast. Truss the chicken. In a small bowl combine the remaining 2 tablespoons butter and the remaining 1 teaspoon garlic. Season the outside of the chicken with salt and pepper and smear with the garlic butter.

5. Scatter the remaining chopped onion and carrot over the bottom of a flameproof roasting pan and place the chicken on top. Lightly cover with aluminum foil. Bake for 1 hour, basting occasionally.

Increase the temperature to 400°F/180°C and bake for 15 minutes more, without foil covering, basting every 5 to 10 minutes.

6. When the skin is browned and crisp, transfer the chicken to a warmed serving plate. The internal temperature should be 180° F/82°C. Tent with aluminum foil to keep warm.

7. Place the roasting pan over medium heat and cook until the juices caramelize on the bottom and separate from the fat. Spoon off all but 2 tablespoons fat. Sprinkle the vegetables with the flour and cook, stirring, for 3 minutes. Add the wine and vinegar and scrape up any browned bits from the bottom of the pan, stirring to dissolve them. Reduce the liquid by half.

8. Add the water or chicken stock and any juices from under the resting chicken. Reduce again by one-third. Season with salt and pepper. Strain the gravy into a warmed sauceboat and serve with the chicken. Serve this with a medley of assorted vegetables such as broccoli, zucchini and carrots.

Note: Roasting the chicken first at the lower temperature, then raising it higher for the last 15 minutes, will keep the meat very moist while producing a wonderfully crispy skin.

grilled jamaican jerk chicken breast

YIELD: 4 SERVINGS

JAMAICAN JERK CHICKEN seasoning is a dry seasoning blend that originated on the Caribbean island after which it's named, and which is used primarily in the preparation of grilled meat. The ingredients can vary, depending on the cook, but the Jamaican jerk blend is generally a combination of chilies, thyme, spices (such as cinnamon, ginger, allspice and cloves), garlic and onions. Jerk seasoning can either be rubbed directly onto meat, or blended with a liquid to create a marinade. In the Caribbean, the most common meats seasoned in this fashion are pork and chicken.

I suggest serving this dish with black beans and rice. And using 10-minute rice is quick and easy. Once you add the rice to the water, add the black beans at the same time and wow, in ten minutes, you have a great side dish.

4 BONELESS, SKINLESS CHICKEN BREASTS, 6 TO 8 OUNCES (170-226 G) EACH

1/2 CUP (125 ML) VEGETABLE OIL

1 MEDIUM ONION, COARSELY CHOPPED

2 SCALLIONS, COARSELY CHOPPED

1 LARGE SCOTCH BONNET CHILI PEPPER, STEMMED AND SEEDED (SEE NOTE, BELOW)

1 TABLESPOON GRATED FRESH GINGER

3 CLOVES GARLIC, COARSELY CHOPPED

1 TABLESPOON FINELY CHOPPED FRESH THYME

2 TABLESPOONS RED WINE VINEGAR

1 TABLESPOON LIGHTLY PACKED LIGHT BROWN SUGAR

1/4 TEASPOON GROUND CINNAMON

1/4 TEASPOON FRESHLY GRATED NUTMEG

PINCH GROUND CLOVES

1 TEASPOON GROUND ALLSPICE

1/2 TEASPOON SALT

1/4 TEASPOON FRESHLY GROUND BLACK PEPPER

1 TEASPOON FRESH LIME JUICE

CHOPPED SCALLIONS FOR GARNISH

1. Pierce the chicken breasts all over with the tines of a fork and place in a large shallow baking dish. In a food processor, combine the remaining ingredients and purée until almost smooth. Pour the mixture over the chicken and rub it in. Cover and refrigerate, turning occasionally, for 24 to 48 hours (the longer the marinade time, the stronger the final flavor).

2. Heat a charcoal or gas grill to medium hot. Remove the chicken from the marinade and pat dry with paper towels. Grill until cooked through, about 5 minutes on each side. To serve, sprinkle with chopped scallions.

Note: The Scotch bonnet chili pepper is one of the hottest chilies on earth. Wash your hands immediately after handling it so that you don't inadvertently touch your eyes with the chilies' oil on your fingers. Better yet, wear rubber gloves while seeding and chopping.

chicken fricassée floridiana

entrées

FRICASSÉE is a dish of meat, usually chicken, that has been sautéed in butter before being stewed with vegetables and herbs. The end result is a thick, chunky, flavorful stew, often flavored with wine.

1 WHOLE CHICKEN (2½ TO 3 POUNDS) (1-1.4 KG), QUARTERED

SALT AND FRESHLY GROUND BLACK PEPPER TO TASTE

5 TABLESPOONS EXTRA-VIRGIN OLIVE OIL

1 CUP (140 G) FINELY CHOPPED YELLOW ONION

2 MEDIUM CARROTS, CHOPPED

4 CLOVES GARLIC, MINCED

1 CUP (250 ML) CHICKEN STOCK (PAGE 152)

½ CUP (124 ML) FRESH ORANGE JUICE

½ CUP (124 ML) CANNED CRUSHED TOMATOES

1 TABLESPOON DRIED ROSEMARY

1 MEDIUM RED BELL PEPPER, CORED, SEEDED, AND CUT INTO JULIENNE STRIPS

1 MEDIUM ZUCCHINI, SLICED DIAGONALLY

1 MEDIUM YELLOW SQUASH, SLICED DIAGONALLY

⅓ CUP (50 G) CHOPPED FRESH ITALIAN PARSLEY

GRATED ZEST OF 1 ORANGE

1. Rinse the chicken pieces with cold water and pat dry with paper towels. Season with salt and pepper. In a nonreactive skillet, heat 3 tablespoons oil over medium-high heat. Add half the chicken pieces, skin side down, and sauté just until pale gold, about 5 minutes on each side (do not try to brown the chicken). Transfer to a flameproof casserole or Dutch oven. Repeat with the remaining chicken pieces.

2. Add the onion, carrots and garlic to the skillet and reduce the heat to low. Cook, covered, until the vegetables soften, about 25 minutes. Stir in the chicken stock, orange juice, tomatoes and rosemary. Season with salt and pepper. Increase the heat to medium and bring to a simmer. Cook, uncovered, for 15 minutes. Transfer the contents of the skillet to the casserole.

3. Bring the fricassée to a boil over medium heat. Reduce the heat to low and gently simmer, stirring occasionally, for 20 to 25 minutes, basting the chicken with the sauce and turning once after 15 minutes.

4. Meanwhile, in a clean skillet, heat the remaining 2 tablespoons oil over medium heat. Add the bell pepper and sauté for 5 minutes. Add the zucchini and squash and season with salt and pepper. Increase the heat to medium-high and cook, stirring, until the vegetables are tender but still firm, about 5 minutes.

5. With a slotted spoon, transfer the vegetables to the fricassée and simmer for 5 minutes. Sprinkle with the chopped parsley and orange zest and serve immediately.

roast pork
with fennel

entrées

3 TABLESPOONS UNSALTED BUTTER

1 TABLESPOON EXTRA-VIRGIN OLIVE OIL

1 TABLESPOON FINELY CHOPPED GARLIC

1 TEASPOON FINELY CHOPPED FRESH ROSEMARY

1 TEASPOON FENNEL SEEDS, LIGHTLY CRUSHED

SALT AND FRESHLY GROUND BLACK PEPPER TO TASTE

1 3 1/2-POUND (1.5 KG) PORK LOIN, BONES SPLIT BY THE BUTCHER

1 LARGE BULB FENNEL, TRIMMED AND ROUGHLY CHOPPED

1/2 CUP (125 ML) WHOLE MILK

1 TABLESPOON ALL-PURPOSE FLOUR

1 CUP (250 ML) DRY WHITE WINE

1. Preheat the oven to 375°F/190°C. Coat the bottom of a flame-proof roasting pan with 1 tablespoon butter and the oil. In a small bowl, combine the garlic, rosemary, fennel seeds, salt and pepper. Rub the seasoning mixture all over the pork loin and place the loin, fat side up, in the prepared roasting pan.

2. Roast the pork loin, uncovered, for 1 1/2 hours, or until a meat thermometer registers 150°F/70°C. Transfer to a warmed serving platter and tent with aluminum foil to keep warm. Let rest for 15 minutes. Reserve the roasting pan and its juices.

3. Meanwhile, in a saucepan, bring the chopped fennel, remaining 2 tablespoons butter and 1 cup (250 ml) water to a boil over medium heat. Reduce the heat to low and cook, covered, until tender. Transfer the contents of the pan to a food processor and add the milk. Purée until slightly chunky. Return the sauce to the saucepan and reserve.

4. Place the roasting pan over medium heat and cook until the juices caramelize on the bottom and separate from the fat. Spoon off all but 1 tablespoon fat. Add the flour and cook, stirring, for 1 minute. Whisk in the wine and any juices from under the resting pork. Scrape up any browned bits from the bottom of the pan and stir to dissolve them. Bring to a simmer and cook, stirring, until thickened.

5. Strain the pan juices through a fine sieve into the fennel sauce and place over low heat. Cook, stirring, just until heated through. Season with salt and pepper. To serve, slice the pork loin and serve the sauce in a warmed sauceboat on the side.

grilled herbed pork chops

FRESH PORK is available year-round. Look for pork that is pale pink with a small amount of marbling and white (not yellow) fat. The darker pink the flesh, the older the animal. Fresh pork that will be used within six hours of purchase may be refrigerated in its store packaging. Otherwise, remove the packaging and store loosely wrapped with waxed paper in the coldest part of the refrigerator for up to two days. Wrapped airtight, pork can be frozen from three to six months, with the larger cuts having longer freezerlife than chops or ground meat. Great to serve with our special Royal Culinary Collections™ Cococay Barbeque Sauce.

4 8-OUNCE (226 G) PORK LOIN CHOPS

1/4 CUP (60 ML) EXTRA-VIRGIN OLIVE OIL

2 TABLESPOONS CHOPPED FRESH SAGE

1 TABLESPOON CHOPPED FRESH THYME

1 TABLESPOON CHOPPED FRESH ROSEMARY

1 BAY LEAF, CRUMBLED

1 CLOVE GARLIC, MINCED

SALT AND FRESHLY GROUND BLACK PEPPER TO TASTE

1 LEMON, QUARTERED

ASSORTED PEPPERS FOR GARNISH

ROSEMARY SPRIGS FOR GARNISH

1. Arrange the pork chops in a single layer in a large shallow baking dish. In a small bowl, combine the remaining ingredients except the lemon and rosemary sprig. Pour the mixture over the chops, cover and refrigerate, turning 3 to 4 times, for 12 hours.

2. Heat a charcoal grill or broiler. Remove the chops from the marinade and pat dry with paper towels. Season with salt and pepper. Grill until cooked through but still slightly pink inside, about 10 minutes on each side. Garnish with assorted peppers and rosemary sprigs. Serve immediately.

mediterranean pork ragôut

YIELD: 4 TO 6 SERVINGS

entrées

"**RAGÔUT**" is a derivative of the French word "*ragoûter*," meaning to stimulate the appetite. It is a thick, rich, well-seasoned stew of meat, poultry or fish. A ragout can be made with or without fruits and/or vegetables. In this case pork is used and it is combined with dried fruits, honey and fresh herbs.

3 POUNDS (1.3 KG) BONELESS PORK, CUT INTO 1-INCH (2.5 CM) CUBES

24 DRIED APRICOT HALVES

1 CUP (140 G) DARK SEEDLESS RAISINS

1 CUP (250 ML) DRY RED WINE

1 CUP (250 ML) RED WINE VINEGAR

3 TABLESPOONS CHOPPED FRESH DILL

3 TABLESPOONS CHOPPED FRESH MINT

1 TEASPOON GROUND CUMIN

1 TEASPOON FRESHLY GROUND BLACK PEPPER

1 TABLESPOON DRIED THYME

SALT TO TASTE

1/3 CUP (75 ML) EXTRA-VIRGIN OLIVE OIL

4 MEDIUM SHALLOTS, MINCED

1 CUP (250 ML) DRY WHITE WINE

1 QUART (1 L) CHICKEN STOCK (SEE PAGE 152)

2 BAY LEAVES

1/4 CUP (60 ML) HONEY

1. In a large nonreactive bowl, combine the pork, apricots, raisins, red wine, vinegar, dill, mint, cumin, pepper, thyme and salt. Toss to coat. Cover, place in the refrigerator, and let marinate for 24 hours, stirring occasionally.

2. Remove the pork from the marinade and pat dry with paper towels. Remove the apricots and raisins and reserve them in a small bowl. Reserve the marinade separately.

3. In a large heavy skillet or cast-iron pan, heat the oil over medium-high heat. Add the pork, in batches, and brown on all sides. With a slotted spoon, transfer to a flameproof casserole or Dutch oven.

4. Drain most of the oil from the skillet and add the shallots. Sauté over medium heat for 5 minutes. Add the reserved marinade and bring to a boil. Scrape up any browned bits from the bottom of the skillet and stir to dissolve them. Bring to a simmer and cook, stirring, until slightly reduced, about 3 minutes. Transfer to the casserole.

5. Preheat the oven to 350°F/180°C. Place the casserole over medium heat. Add the reserved fruit, 1/2 cup (125 ml) white wine, 2 cups (500 ml) chicken stock, bay leaves and honey. Bring to a boil, cover, and transfer to the oven. Bake for 1 hour and 15 minutes. Uncover and check the consistency: if the meat seems too dry, add additional wine and stock. Return to the oven and bake, uncovered, for 30 to 45 minutes more, or until the meat is tender and the sauce rich and thick. Remove the bay leaves before serving.

Note: I like to serve this dish with wild rice.

rack of lamb
with spring vegetables

entrées

As noted below, this recipe calls for a "frenched" lamb rack. This technique is a little complicated, so ask your butcher to trim and french the lamb for you.

Lamb Rack

3 RACKS OF LAMB WITH 8 CHOPS EACH, FRENCHED

2 STICKS (240 G) UNSALTED BUTTER

3 TABLESPOONS DIJON MUSTARD

2 TEASPOONS FRESH THYME LEAVES

1 TABLESPOON CHOPPED FRESH MARJORAM

1 TABLESPOON CHOPPED FRESH PARSLEY

3 CLOVES GARLIC, CHOPPED

SALT AND FRESHLY GROUND BLACK PEPPER TO TASTE

1. Trim the lamb of any excess fat and set aside. In a small saucepan, melt the butter over low heat. Cook until the butterfat becomes clear and the milk solids drop to the bottom of the pan. Skim the surface foam as the butter separates. Carefully spoon the clear butterfat into a medium bowl. Discard the milky liquid at the bottom of the saucepan.

2. Add the remaining ingredients to the butter and stir to combine. Brush the lamb with the mixture, cover with plastic wrap, and marinate in the refrigerator for 4 hours.

Tomato Provençal

4 RIPE MEDIUM TOMATOES, PEELED, SEEDED AND CHOPPED
(SEE CONCASSÉ, IN BASIC KNIFE TECHNIQUES, PAGE 12)

1/4 CUP (60 ML) EXTRA-VIRGIN OLIVE OIL

3 CLOVES GARLIC, CHOPPED

1 TEASPOON FRESH THYME LEAVES

SALT AND FRESHLY GROUND BLACK PEPPER TO TASTE

2 TABLESPOONS CHOPPED FRESH PARSLEY

In a nonreactive skillet, heat the oil over medium-high heat. Add the tomatoes and cook, stirring, for 30 seconds. Add the garlic and thyme and bring to a simmer. Season with salt and pepper. Cook, stirring, until quite thick. Stir in the parsley, remove from the heat, and let cool. Reserve.

Vegetable Garnish

12 BABY CARROTS, SCRUBBED AND TRIMMED

6 BABY TURNIPS, SCRUBBED AND TRIMMED

36 HARICOTS VERTS (THIN GREEN BEANS), ENDS TRIMMED

2 CUPS (280 G) FRESH SHELLED PEAS

12 PEARL ONIONS

2 TABLESPOONS UNSALTED BUTTER

²/₃ CUP (150 ML) DRY WHITE WINE

1. Prepare a bowl of ice water. Bring a large saucepan of salted water to a boil. Add the carrots and turnips and cook until tender, about 7 minutes. Remove with a strainer and shock in the ice water to stop the cooking. Drain and transfer to a bowl. Repeat the procedure with the haricots verts and peas and cook just until bright green and tender-crisp, about 3 minutes. Remove with a strainer and shock in the ice water. Drain and add to the other vegetables.

2. With the water still at a boil, make a small shallow X at the root end of each pearl onion. Add the pearl onions to the boiling water and cook until slightly softened on the outside but still uncooked within. Drain and transfer to the bowl of cold water. Remove the skins, drain, and reserve separately from the other vegetables.

3. In a sauté pan, heat the butter over medium heat. Add the pearl onions and wine and cook, stirring, until the wine is evaporated and the onions are golden. Remove from the heat, add to the other vegetables, and reserve.

To Assemble

3 TABLESPOONS (45 G) UNSALTED BUTTER

SALT AND FRESHLY GROUND BLACK PEPPER TO TASTE

1. Preheat the oven to 425°F/220°C. In a large flameproof roasting pan, heat 1 tablespoon butter over medium heat. When the butter begins to brown, add the lamb racks. Transfer the pan to the oven and roast for 15 minutes.

2. Remove the pan from the oven and heat the broiler. Spread the racks, just on the meat not the bones, with the tomato provençal and broil for 5 minutes, or until medium-rare in the center. Remove from the oven, tent with aluminum foil, and let rest for 10 minutes.

3. To serve, heat the remaining 2 tablespoons butter over medium heat. Add the vegetable garnish and cook, stirring, until heated through. Season with salt and pepper. Cut the racks into chops and divide among 6 warmed plates. Garnish with the vegetables and serve immediately.

garlic-roasted leg of lamb
with natural jus

entrées

YIELD: 4 SERVINGS

Lamb is classified into different categories according to age. They are baby, spring, regular, yearling and mutton. The latter being the oldest (over two years in age) and has a much stronger flavor and less tender flesh. When purchasing lamb, let color be the guide. Personally, I like to ask my butcher, he always knows best! In general, the darker the color, the older the animal. Lamb can be purchased in steak, chops and roasts. Refrigerate ground lamb and small lamb cuts loosely wrapped for up to 3 days. Roasts can be stored up to 5 days.

1 5- TO-6-POUND (2.2-2.7 KG) LEG OF LAMB, TRIMMED OF FAT

12 SMALL CLOVES GARLIC

3 TABLESPOONS EXTRA-VIRGIN OLIVE OIL

1 TABLESPOON MINCED FRESH ROSEMARY

1 TABLESPOON MINCED FRESH THYME

1 TABLESPOON MINCED FRESH OREGANO

SALT AND FRESHLY GROUND BLACK PEPPER TO TASTE

3/4 CUP (100 G) CHOPPED ONION

1/2 CUP (70 G) CHOPPED CELERY

1/3 CUP (50 G) CHOPPED CARROT

1 QUART (1 L) DARK CHICKEN STOCK (SEE PAGE 152)

1. Preheat the oven to 350°F/180°C. Cut 12 slits into the lamb, about 1/2 inch (1.25 cm) in length. Push the garlic cloves into the slits. In a small bowl, combine the oil and herbs and rub the mixture all over the lamb. Season with salt and pepper.

2. Roast the lamb in a large flameproof roasting pan for 1 hour and 45 minutes, or until medium-rare, basting occasionally with the pan juices. (An instant-read thermometer should register 150°F/65°C.) Transfer to a warmed serving platter and tent with aluminum foil to keep warm.

3. Spoon off most of the fat from the roasting pan and leave the natural meat juices behind. Place the pan over medium heat. Add the onion, celery and carrot and cook, stirring, until browned. The meat juices should have caramelized on the bottom of the pan and separated from the fat. Spoon off any fat left in the pan.

4. Add the chicken stock and any juices from under the resting lamb. Scrape up any browned bits from the bottom of the roasting pan and stir to dissolve them. Bring to a simmer and cook, stirring, until the liquid is reduced by one-third. Adjust the seasonings. To serve, strain the juices through a fine sieve lined with cheesecloth into a warmed sauceboat. Serve alongside the lamb.

fillet of sea bass
with tarragon and lemon butter

SEA BASS is a term to describe various saltwater fish, most of which are not members of the bass family. Black sea bass (as is striped bass) is a true bass, but white sea bass, which is generally marketed simply as "sea bass" is actually a member of the drum family. The giant sea bass is related to the grouper family and can weigh as much as 550 pounds (250 kg). It is sometimes mistakenly called both black sea bass and jewfish. Sea bass can be found whole and in steaks or fillets. In general, the flesh is lean to moderately fatty and is suitable for almost any method of cooking including baking, broiling, poaching and sautéing.

1 STICK (120 G) UNSALTED BUTTER, SOFTENED

2 TABLESPOONS CHOPPED FRESH TARRAGON

2 TABLESPOONS FRESH LEMON JUICE

SALT AND FRESHLY GROUND BLACK PEPPER TO TASTE

2 MEDIUM ZUCCHINI, CUT INTO $1/4$-INCH (6 MM) THICK SLICES

2 TABLESPOONS EXTRA-VIRGIN OLIVE OIL

NONSTICK COOKING SPRAY FOR GREASING

4 SEA BASS FILLETS, 6 TO 8 OUNCES (170-226 G) EACH

3 RIPE MEDIUM TOMATOES, CUT INTO $1/4$-INCH (6 MM) THICK SLICES

4 LEMON SLICES

4 SPRIGS FRESH TARRAGON

1. In a small mixing bowl, whisk the butter, tarragon and lemon juice. Season with salt and pepper. Spoon the butter mixture along one edge of a piece of parchment or waxed paper, leaving room on either side. Roll into a cylinder and twist the ends to seal. Refrigerate until firm.

2. Heat a charcoal or gas grill. Brush the zucchini slices on both sides with a little of the oil and grill, turning once, until golden, about 2 minutes on each side. Transfer to a plate lined with paper towels to drain.

3. Preheat the oven to 375°F/190°C. Lightly coat a baking sheet with nonstick spray. In a large sauté pan, heat half the oil over medium heat. Season 2 sea bass fillets with salt and pepper and add them to the pan. Sear briefly on both sides. Transfer in a single layer to the prepared baking sheet. Repeat with the remaining oil and sea bass.

4. As if they were scales, overlap, alternating layers of tomato and grilled zucchini slices on each of the fillets. Season with salt and pepper. Bake for 15 to 20 minutes, or until the fish is opaque yet juicy, about 15 minutes.

5. Transfer the fillets to warmed plates and top each with 2 slices tarragon butter. Garnish with a lemon slice and tarragon sprig and serve immediately.

key west grouper
with ginger-orange sauce

2 TABLESPOONS UNSALTED BUTTER

1 MEDIUM SHALLOT, MINCED

1 TEASPOON MINCED FRESH GINGER

1/2 CUP (125 ML) DRY WHITE WINE

1/2 CUP (125 ML) FRESH ORANGE JUICE

1 1/2 CUPS (375 ML) FISH STOCK (SEE PAGE 154)

2 CUPS (500 ML) HEAVY CREAM

SALT AND FRESHLY GROUND WHITE PEPPER TO TASTE

2 CUPS (500 ML) VEGETABLE OIL FOR FRYING

2 MEDIUM LEEKS, WHITE PARTS ONLY, WASHED AND CUT INTO JULIENNE STRIPS

1/4 CUP (35 G) CORNSTARCH

4 GROUPER FILLETS, 6 TO 8 OUNCES (170-226 G) EACH

1/2 CUP (70 G) ALL-PURPOSE FLOUR

3 TABLESPOONS EXTRA-VIRGIN OLIVE OIL

1 BUNCH CHIVES, FINELY CHOPPED

1. In a medium saucepan, heat the butter over medium heat. Add the shallot and cook, stirring, until softened and translucent. Add the ginger and cook until fragrant. Add the wine, orange juice and fish stock and bring to a boil. Reduce the heat and simmer until the liquid is reduced by half. Add the heavy cream and reduce until the sauce lightly coats the back of a spoon. Season with salt and pepper and keep warm over very low heat.

2. In a wok or heavy saucepan, heat the vegetable oil to 350°F/ 180°C. (If the temperature is correct, a small piece of bread dropped into the oil should float up to the surface almost immediately and brown within 45 seconds.) Pat the leeks dry on paper towels. Dredge in the cornstarch and then toss in a mesh strainer to shake off any excess coating. Deep-fry until golden brown and crispy. Transfer to a plate lined with paper towels to drain.

3. Season 2 grouper fillets with salt and pepper and dredge in the flour. Shake off any excess coating. In a large skillet, heat half the olive oil over medium heat. Add the grouper and sauté until golden brown outside and opaque yet moist inside, about 5 minutes on each side. Transfer to a plate lined with paper towels to drain. Repeat with the remaining olive oil and grouper.

4. To serve, divide the grouper among 4 warmed dinner plates. Spoon some ginger-orange sauce over each fillet and garnish with the chopped chives and fried leeks.

sautéed snapper cabana
with mango-pineapple salsa

entrées

BELIEVE IT OR NOT, there are about 250 species of this saltwater fish, 15 of which can be found in the United States waters from the Gulf of Mexico to the coastal waters of North Carolina. Some of the better known species include the gray snapper, mutton snapper, schoolmaster snapper and yellowtail snapper. By far the best known and most popular is the red snapper, so named because of its reddish-pink skin and red eyes. Its flesh is firm textured and contains very little fat. Red snapper grows to 35 pounds (16 kg) but is most commonly marketed in the 2 to 8 pound (1-3.6 kg) range. The smaller sizes are sold whole, while the larger ones can be purchased in steaks and fillets. Snapper is available year round with the peak season in the summer months.

3/4 CUP (100 G) DICED FRESH RIPE MANGO

3/4 CUP (100 G) DICED FRESH RIPE PINEAPPLE

1/2 CUP (70 G) DICED RED ONION

1/4 CUP (35 G) DICED RED BELL PEPPER

1/4 CUP (35 G) FINELY CHOPPED FRESH CILANTRO

1 JALAPEÑO PEPPER, SEEDED AND MINCED

3 TABLESPOONS FRESH LIME JUICE

SALT AND FRESHLY GROUND BLACK PEPPER TO TASTE

3 TABLESPOONS UNSALTED BUTTER

4 SNAPPER FILLETS, 6 TO 8 OUNCES (170-226 G) EACH

4 SPRIGS CILANTRO FOR GARNISH

1. In a nonreactive bowl, combine the mango, pineapple, onion, bell pepper, cilantro and jalapeño. Add the lime juice and toss to coat. Season with salt and pepper. Reserve.

2. In a large skillet, heat half the butter over medium heat. Season 2 snapper fillets with salt and pepper and add to the skillet. Sauté until golden brown outside and opaque yet juicy inside, about 4 minutes on each side. Transfer to warmed dinner plates. Repeat with the remaining butter and snapper.

3. To serve, top each fillet with some mango-pineapple salsa and garnish with a cilantro sprig.

Note: I suggest serving this dish with black beans and rice and sautéed spinach. For the rice, cook the 10-minute rice as it says on the box, and when you add the rice, add a can of black beans as well. For the spinach, sauté it in a little butter and season with salt and pepper. As an alternative, you should try the Royal Culinary Collections™ Tropical Seafood Seasoning.

broiled lobster tail royale

LOBSTER, the king of the crustacean family, is one of the most desireable and delicate tasting shellfishes available. It has a jointed body and limbs covered with a hard body shell. The most popular variety in the United States is the Maine lobster or American lobster. They are found off the Atlantic coast and are available year round. Try this recipe and I assure you, guests will be coming back for more!

4 COLD-WATER LOBSTER TAILS IN THEIR SHELLS, 6 TO 7 OUNCES (170-200 G) EACH

2 STICKS (240 G) UNSALTED BUTTER

2 TEASPOONS FINELY MINCED GARLIC

2 TABLESPOONS FRESH LEMON JUICE

2 TABLESPOONS CHOPPED FRESH PARSLEY

SALT AND FRESHLY GROUND BLACK PEPPER TO TASTE

1. Heat the broiler. With kitchen scissors, cut the upper shell of each lobster tail down the center of the back, leaving the tail fan intact. Lift the uncooked tail meat through the slit so it rests on the shell.

2. In a medium saucepan, melt the butter over medium heat. Add the garlic, lemon juice and parsley. Season with salt and pepper. Cook, without allowing the butter to brown, until the garlic is fragrant. Remove from the heat and keep warm.

3. Place the lobster tails on a broiler pan. Pour 2 tablespoons of the garlic-parsley butter in a small bowl and use it to brush on the lobster tails. Broil the tails, at least 6 inches (15 cm) from the heat, for 8 minutes, or until the meat is opaque and firm to the touch.

4. To serve, place the lobster tails on 4 warmed plates. Divide the warm garlic-parsley butter among 4 ramekins and serve with the lobster for dipping.

Note: I recommend serving this with white rice and steamed broccoli. It is simple yet elegant.

side dishes

I ALWAYS THOUGHT it would be a great idea to open a restaurant that served nothing but side dishes. In fact, I often find myself in an elegant restaurant, menu in hand, only to find that the side dishes are much more appealing and interesting than the entrées. ⚓ ALWAYS CHOOSE YOUR SIDE DISHES to highlight and complement some aspect of the main component of the meal, whether it's meat, fish, fowl or game. In this chapter, you'll find recipes for six smashing sides, each designed to complement a variety of different entrées. The Roasted Garlic Mashed Potatoes, for instance, would be a wonderful accompaniment to a roast of any kind, to absorb the lovely gravy. Fish broiled simply would be well complemented by the Mixed Vegetable Casserole. If you're serving fish or seafood prepared in a more exotic way, with a sauce perhaps, consider a milder side dish such as Baked Carrots. (Remember, the bland color of most fish calls for a side that adds a splash of color to the plate.) Caramelized Brussels Sprouts with Red Onion have the deep, full flavor that you'll want to match a milder meat such as pork or veal.

VISION OF
THE SEAS

roasted garlic
mashed potatoes

THESE ARE MY ALL-TIME FAVORITE mashed potatoes. My family and I eat these at least once a week, usually on Sundays with our roast chicken. For a more rustic taste, substitute the russet potatoes with Red Bliss. Leave the skins on them and follow the recipe as is. You will be amazed at how good they taste!

1 LARGE HEAD GARLIC

1 TABLESPOON EXTRA-VIRGIN OLIVE OIL

SALT AND FRESHLY GROUND BLACK PEPPER TO TASTE

2 SPRIGS ROSEMARY

1 1/2 POUNDS (679 G) RUSSET POTATOES, PEELED AND QUARTERED

3/4 CUP (200 ML) WHOLE MILK, HEATED

1. To roast the garlic, preheat the oven to 325°F/160°C. Pull the papery husk off the garlic head. Slice the tip off the head to expose the cloves. Rub with the oil and season with salt and pepper. Place in an ovenproof dish with the rosemary, sprinkle with a bit of water, and cover with aluminum foil. Roast for 30 to 45 minutes, or until very tender. Let cool. Squeeze the garlic pulp from the skins into a bowl and reserve.

2. Meanwhile, in a large saucepan, combine the potatoes and enough cold water to cover. Add 1 teaspoon salt; bring to a boil. Reduce the heat and simmer for 30 minutes. Drain the potatoes and return them to the saucepan over low heat, to evaporate the small amount of water remaining.

3. Transfer the potatoes to a warmed bowl and mash with a potato masher. Stir the reserved garlic pulp into the heated milk and blend the mixture into the potatoes. Season with salt and pepper and serve immediately.

oven-roasted potatoes

6 LARGE POTATOES, QUARTERED

1/3 CUP (75 ML) VEGETABLE OIL

1 TEASPOON BLACK PEPPER

1 TABLESPOON FRESH PARSLEY, CHOPPED

1 TABLESPOON FRESH BASIL, CHOPPED

1. Preheat the oven to 375° F/190°C.

2. Place the potatoes in a shallow roasting pan.

3. Combine the oil and herbs and pour over the vegetables. Toss to coat.

4. Bake uncovered for 1 hour, or until fork tender.

5. Turn occasionally to prevent sticking.

glazed onions

YIELD: 6 TO 8 SERVINGS

1 1/2 POUNDS (679 G) SMALL WHITE PEARL ONIONS OR 1 16-OUNCE (450 G) JAR

4 TABLESPOONS UNSALTED BUTTER, MELTED

1 CUP (250 ML) CHICKEN STOCK (PAGE 152)

2 TABLESPOONS GRANULATED SUGAR

1/2 TEASPOON SALT

1. Bring a saucepan of salted water to a boil. With a paring knife, make a small shallow X at the root end of each onion. Add the onions to the boiling water and cook until slightly softened on the outside but still uncooked within. Drain and transfer to a bowl of cool water. Remove the skins and transfer the onions to a medium saucepan.

2. Add the butter to the onions and place over low heat. Cook, stirring, until the onions are coated with the butter. Add the remaining ingredients and cook very slowly, stirring occasionally, until the onions are tender and the liquid is completely reduced, about 20 minutes. Serve with roast beef or chicken.

Note: To make life easier, I suggest using a jar of pearl onions. They can be found in the canned vegetable section of your local supermarket. Step one of this recipe can be completely avoided and time will be saved!

baked carrots

YIELD: 6 SERVINGS

BAKED CARROTS are very versatile; you can serve them with meat, poultry, fish or pork. Personally, I like to serve them alongside a roast chicken or turkey, especially during the holidays.

2 POUNDS (905 G) CARROTS, SLICED ON THE BIAS INTO
1/4-INCH-THICK (6 MM) ROUNDS

1 TABLESPOON EXTRA-VIRGIN OLIVE OIL

1/2 CUP (70 G) DICED ONION

1 TABLESPOON CHOPPED FRESH THYME LEAVES

1/2 CUP (125 ML) CHICKEN STOCK (PAGE 152)

2 TABLESPOONS PURE MAPLE SYRUP

1 TABLESPOON CHOPPED FRESH DILL

1. Preheat the oven to 375°F/190°C. Bring a medium saucepan of salted water to a boil. Add the carrots and cook just until tender-crisp, about 4 minutes. Drain and set aside.

2. In a sauté pan, heat the oil over medium-high heat. Add the onion and cook, stirring, until softened and translucent. Add the thyme and cook for 2 minutes more. Stir in the chicken stock and maple syrup.

3. Add the cooked carrots and toss to coat. Transfer the contents of the pan to an ovenproof serving dish. Sprinkle with the dill and bake, covered, for 10 minutes. Serve immediately.

caramelized brussels sprouts
and red onions

YIELD: 6 SERVINGS

side dishes

2 10-OUNCE (290 G) CONTAINERS BRUSSELS SPROUTS

1 10-OUNCE (290 G) CONTAINER RED PEARL ONIONS

2 TABLESPOONS UNSALTED BUTTER

SALT AND FRESHLY GROUND BLACK PEPPER TO TASTE

1. In a large saucepan, bring 1$\frac{1}{2}$ inches (3.75 cm) salted water to a boil. Remove the wilted outer leaves from the sprouts. With a paring knife, trim away any brown coloring from the stem ends and make a small shallow X there. Wash well and drain.

2. Add the sprouts to the boiling water and cook, covered, at a low boil just until tender, about 8 minutes. Drain and transfer to a bowl of cold water to stop the cooking. Drain again and set aside.

3. Meanwhile, in a medium saucepan, bring 1 inch (2.5 cm) salted water to a boil. With a paring knife, make a small shallow X at the root end of each pearl onion. Add the pearl onions to the boiling water and cook, half covered, at a low boil just until tender, about 4 to 6 minutes. Drain and transfer to the bowl of cold water. Remove the skins and set aside.

4. In a large skillet, heat the butter over medium-high heat. Add the sprouts and cook, without stirring, until the sprouts start to brown, about 3 to 4 minutes. (At this point, the sprouts can be stirred.) Add the onions and cook, stirring, until the vegetables are heated through. Season with salt and pepper and serve immediately.

mixed vegetable casserole

YIELD: 4 SERVINGS

1 TEASPOON EXTRA-VIRGIN
OLIVE OIL

1/4 CUP (70 G) MINCED
WHITE ONION

1/4 POUND (112 G) WHITE
MUSHROOMS, WIPED CLEAN
AND QUARTERED

12 BABY CARROTS, SCRUBBED

1 RED BELL PEPPER, CORED,
SEEDED AND CUT INTO
JULIENNE STRIPS

1 GREEN BELL PEPPER, CORED,
SEEDED AND CUT INTO
JULIENNE STRIPS

2 TABLESPOONS CHOPPED GARLIC

1 TABLESPOON CHOPPED FRESH
THYME LEAVES

1 SMALL ZUCCHINI, SLICED INTO
1/4-INCH-THICK (6 MM) ROUNDS

1 SMALL YELLOW SQUASH,
SLICED INTO 1/4-INCH (6 MM)
ROUNDS

1 VERY SMALL EGGPLANT,
HALVED LENGTHWISE AND
SLICED INTO 1/4-INCH (6 MM)
HALF-MOONS

1 CUP (250 ML) CHICKEN STOCK
(PAGE 152)

4 RIPE MEDIUM TOMATOES,
PEELED, SEEDED AND CHOPPED

1. In a Dutch oven, heat the oil over medium-high heat. Add the onion and cook, stirring, until softened and translucent. Add the mushrooms, carrots and bell peppers. Cook, stirring, for 2 minutes. Add the garlic and thyme and cook until the garlic becomes fragrant.

2. Add the zucchini, squash, eggplant and chicken stock. Reduce the heat to low and cook, covered, until the vegetables are tender, about 15 minutes.

3. See Basic Knife Techniques (page 12) on how to concassé tomatoes.

4. Add the tomatoes to the vegetables and cook, stirring, for 5 minutes more. Serve immediately.

Note: I like to serve this on top of white rice alongside of the Roast Pork with Fennel.

desserts

NOTHING ELICITS EXCITEMENT at the table the way a spectacular dessert does. After the meal, memories of dessert are the ones that seem to last longest. On our ships, we often hear passengers discussing dessert as soon as they sit down to eat, planning the rest of their meal around it. Dessert carries a powerful emotional component for both kids and adults. It conjures up evocative childhood memories: of cookies baking and pies in the oven, of cinnamon and nutmeg, of butter and warm chocolate, of fruit picked fresh from the tree. I PREFER DESSERTS that are straightforward, homey and comforting. Since dessert should be pure pleasure, in the making as well as the eating, I've selected recipes made from easy to find ingredients and simple techniques. The results are guaranteed to bring a grin to every face at your table. ARE YOU A DEVOTEE OF FRUIT DESSERTS? There are plenty of them here, including Banana-Pistachio Strudel with Rum-Raisin Sauce. There are cakes and cheesecakes that could win ribbons in any county fair. You'll also find a classic Crème Brulee, an elegant mainstay of French restaurants everywhere, flavored perfectly with raspberry. Raspberry pops up again in a Tiramisu, another "ethnic" dessert that has recently gone mainstream. In fact, I love to take classic desserts and enhance them with fruit flavors, such as my Blueberry Bread-and-Butter Pudding. IF YOU'RE ONE OF THOSE PEOPLE who believes dessert isn't dessert unless it's chocolate, you'll love the recipe for Flourless Chocolate Cake. The Aztecs believed that chocolate was sent from heaven, and this rich, dense cake has been known to induce religious-like reverence. Known in France as *Gâteau Chocolat Sans Farine*, it's rumored to be the happy result of a simple mistake in the pastry kitchen. Similar to a fluffy souffle, the cake is made with egg whites, egg yolks, sugar and chocolate. OR, WHY NOT SET OUT to really dazzle your guests with Crêpes Suzette? These are two classic "fancy" desserts that were standard on continental menus from the 1930s to the 1960s and are still huge favorites on our ships today. Whichever you choose, just make sure that your dessert is drop-dead delicious...and make sure that you prepare enough. These recipes are guaranteed to make everyone scream for seconds.

GRANDEUR OF THE SEAS

carrot cake

4 MEDIUM EGGS

1 1/4 CUPS (310 G) VEGETABLE OIL

2 CUPS (280 G) GRANULATED SUGAR

2 CUPS (280 G) PLUS 1 TABLESPOON ALL-PURPOSE FLOUR

1 1/2 TEASPOONS GROUND CINNAMON

3/4 TEASPOON BAKING SODA

1/4 TEASPOON BAKING POWDER

1/8 TEASPOON SALT

2 CUPS (280 G) PEELED AND GRATED CARROTS

1 1/4 CUPS (175 G) CHOPPED WALNUTS

1 CUP (140 G) PLUS 1 TABLESPOON CREAM CHEESE, SOFTENED

4 TABLESPOONS UNSALTED BUTTER, SOFTENED

1/2 CUP (70 G) CONFECTIONERS' SUGAR

1. Preheat the oven to 350°F/180°C. Coat two 9-inch (22.5 cm) cake pans with butter. Dust the pans with a little flour; tilt to coat and tap out the excess.

2. Crack the eggs into a medium bowl. With an electric mixer, beat at medium speed until lightly beaten. With the mixer running, gradually add the oil. Reduce the speed to low and beat in the sugar until smooth.

3. In a large bowl, combine the flour, cinnamon, baking soda, baking powder and salt. Make a well in the center of the dry ingredients. Add the wet ingredients from above and stir until just combined. With a rubber spatula, carefully fold in the carrots and 1/4 cup (35 g) walnuts.

4. Divide the batter evenly between the prepared pans and bake for 35 to 45 minutes, or until a skewer inserted in the center of each comes out clean. Transfer the pans to a wire rack and let cool completely. Run a knife around the edge of each pan and turn the cakes out onto the rack.

5. In a medium bowl, beat the cream cheese, butter and confectioners' sugar until smooth. With a serrated knife, level the tops of the cake layers if necessary and cut each cake in half to make 2 layers each. Stack the 4 layers, spreading some of the cream cheese mixture between the layers and on the sides. Press the remaining walnuts onto the sides of the cake and frost the top of the cake with the remaining cream cheese mixture. Cover with plastic wrap and chill in the refrigerator before serving.

Note: Raisins are a good addition to this recipe. One cup (140 g) of raisins may be added to the batter at the same time as the walnuts and carrots.

banana-pistachio strudel
with rum-raisin sauce

YIELD: 6 SERVINGS

Rum-Raisin Sauce

1/3 CUP (50 G) SUGAR

1/2 CUP (125 ML) SPICED RUM

1/2 CUP (70 G) RAISINS

1 QUART (1 L) WHOLE MILK

1/2 TEASPOON PURE VANILLA EXTRACT

3 LARGE EGG YOLKS

1. Gently warm the rum in a small saucepan over medium heat or in the microwave on medium power. In a small bowl, combine with the raisins. Marinate for at least 30 minutes.

2. In a medium saucepan, bring the milk and vanilla to a boil.

3. Meanwhile, in a mixing bowl, whisk the egg yolks and sugar until pale in color. Slowly pour half of the boiling milk mixture into the egg yolk mixture, gently whisking until well blended.

4. Prepare a large bowl of ice water. Return the egg yolk mixture to the saucepan and place over medium-low heat. Gently cook, stirring continually with a wooden spoon, until the mixture thickens and coats the back of the spoon and an instant-read thermometer registers 185°F/85°C. (The mixture should not be allowed to boil.) Immediately remove the mixture from the heat and strain through a fine sieve into a medium bowl. Place the bowl in the larger bowl of ice water to chill the sauce down quickly and prevent curdling.

5. When the mixture is cool, stir in the rum-raisin marinade. Cover with plastic wrap and chill in the refrigerator until ready to use.

Strudel

1/2 CUP (70 G) PISTACHIO NUTS, SHELLED

4 SHEETS PHYLLO DOUGH (18 BY 14 INCHES) (45 X 35 CM)

1 STICK (120 G) UNSALTED BUTTER, MELTED

2 TABLESPOONS GRANULATED SUGAR

1/2 CUP (70 G) YELLOW OR WHITE CAKE CRUMBS

5 RIPE BANANAS, PEELED AND SPLIT LENGTHWISE

2 TABLESPOONS SPICED RUM

1. Preheat the oven to 350°F/180°C. Spread the pistachios on a baking sheet and bake for 5 to 7 minutes. Let cool, chop and set aside. Increase the oven temperature to 385°F/195°C. Lightly butter the baking sheet.

2. Lay 1 sheet of phyllo on a work surface. (Keep the remaining phyllo covered with plastic wrap and a damp kitchen towel.) With a pastry brush, brush the phyllo sheet lightly with some melted butter. Sprinkle with one-fourth of the sugar and one-fourth of the cake crumbs. Lay another sheet of phyllo on top. Lightly brush with more butter and sprinkle with more sugar and cake crumbs. Repeat with the remaining 2 sheets of phyllo.

3. Arrange some of the sliced bananas along 1 long edge of the phyllo so that the bananas cover an 18-by-3 inch (45 x 7.5 cm) area. Sprinkle the bananas with some pistachios and the spiced rum. Top the bananas with any remaining bananas and pistachios.

4. Starting from the banana-lined edge, roll up the phyllo into a cylinder. Place the strudel on the prepared baking sheet and brush with melted butter. Bake for 10 minutes, or until the pastry is crisp on the outside and warm on the inside.

5. To serve, transfer the strudel to a cutting board and slice into 6 diagonal slices. Serve with the rum-raisin sauce on top.

blueberry
bread-and-butter pudding

BREAD PUDDING is a simple, delicious dessert made with cubes or slices of bread saturated with a mixture of milk, eggs, sugar, vanilla and spices. In this case, the bread is buttered before being added to the liquid mixture. This is what classifies it as a bread and butter pudding. Traditionally this dish is served warm, usually with cream or a dessert sauce.

$^1/_2$ LOAF BRIOCHE OR
1 POUND (454 G) CHALLAH
(SWEET EGG BREAD)

2 CUPS (500 ML) MILK

2 CUPS (500 ML) HEAVY CREAM

PINCH SALT

1 VANILLA BEAN, SPLIT

6 LARGE EGGS

1 CUP (140 G) GRANULATED
SUGAR

2 CUPS (280 G) BLUEBERRIES

$^1/_4$ CUP (35 G) CONFECTIONERS
SUGAR

4 TABLESPOONS BUTTER,
SOFTENED

1. Preheat the oven to 350°F/180°C. Cut the crusts from the brioche (or challah) and cut the bread into cubes. Place the bread cubes on a baking sheet and toast in the oven until golden brown. Remove the bread from the oven and place into a bowl. Melt the butter and toss with the toasted bread cubes, reserve.

2. In a medium saucepan, slowly bring the milk, cream and salt to a boil over medium-low heat. Reduce the heat to low. Use the tip of a blunt knife to scrape the vanilla bean seeds into the cream. Gently simmer, stirring occasionally, until the vanilla has infused the cream, about 15 minutes.

3. In a mixing bowl, whisk the eggs and granulated sugar until pale in color. Slowly add the vanilla-infused cream and whisk until well blended. Strain through a fine sieve into a larger bowl. Add the bread cubes to the bowl and toss to coat. Set aside for 20 minutes.

4. Meanwhile, bring a large kettle of water to a boil. Line a small roasting pan with a folded kitchen towel. Place six 8-ounce (226 g) soufflé dishes or ramekins in the roasting pan. Butter the sides and bottom of the ramekins and sprinkle with sugar. Divide the blueberries among the soufflé dishes and top with the soaked bread. Top off the dishes with any remaining custard.

5. Pour enough boiling water into the roasting pan to come halfway up the sides of the dishes. Bake for 45 to 50 minutes, or until set and golden brown. Remove the dishes from the oven and let cool slightly on a wire rack. Place the confectioners' sugar in a sieve and sprinkle it over the tops of the puddings. Serve immediately.

desserts

cheesecake

ALTHOUGH CHEESECAKES MAY BE SAVORY, most of us think of them as being luscious, rich desserts. The main ingredients include cream cheese, ricotta cheese or cottage cheese, usually creamed together with eggs, sugar and other flavorings. The mixture is then poured into a special springform pan and baked. Once finished they may be topped with an assortment of fresh fruits or whipped cream.

Crust

2 CUPS (280 G) GRAHAM CRACKER CRUMBS

1/2 CUP (70 G) PLUS 1 TABLESPOON GRANULATED SUGAR

4 TABLESPOONS UNSALTED BUTTER, MELTED

1 LARGE EGG WHITE, LIGHTLY BEATEN

Preheat the oven to 375°F/ 190°C. In a medium bowl, mix together all the ingredients. Press into the bottom and sides of a 10-inch (25 cm) springform cake pan. Bake for 5 to 7 minutes, or until the crust is golden. Remove from the oven and bring to room temperature. Cover with plastic wrap and chill in the refrigerator until ready to use.

Filling

2 1/2 POUNDS (1.2 KG) CREAM CHEESE, SOFTENED

1 3/4 CUPS (240 G) GRANULATED SUGAR

2 LARGE EGGS

1 TABLESPOON FRESH LEMON JUICE

1 TABLESPOON PURE VANILLA EXTRACT

2/3 CUP (150 ML) HEAVY CREAM

Garnish

1 CUP (140 G) BLUEBERRIES

1 CUP (140 G) STRAWBERRIES, SLICED

1 CUP (140 G) BLACKBERRIES

1/2 CUP (70 G) MANGO PURÉE

1. Reduce the oven temperature to 300°F/150°C. Bring a large kettle of water to a boil. Wrap the outside of the crust-lined cake pan with a double thickness of aluminum foil to prevent water from seeping in.

2. In a large mixing bowl, combine the cream cheese and sugar. With an electric mixer, beat at medium speed until

smooth. In a small bowl, lightly beat the eggs, lemon juice and vanilla. With the mixer running, add the egg mixture to the cream cheese mixture in 4 increments, beating well and scraping the bowl after each addition. Add the heavy cream and mix well.

3. Pour the cream cheese mixture into the prepared crust and place the cheesecake in a shallow roasting pan. Pour enough boiling water into the roasting pan to come 1/2 inch (1.25 cm) up the outside of the cake pan. Bake for 60 to 90 minutes, or until the edges are set and the center is firm. Remove the cheesecake from the oven and let cool on a wire rack. Cover with plastic wrap and refrigerate until chilled.

4. Serve topped with an assortment of blueberries, strawberries, blackberries and mango purée.

Note: Any combination of your favorite berries or fruit purée may be used for this recipe.

crêpes suzette

THIS ILLUSTRIOUS DESSERT consists of an orange butter sauce in which the crêpes are warmed, then doused with Grand Marnier and ignited to flaming glory. This is a great dessert to serve during the holidays when many people are gathered around to watch in amazement! But please be careful; do not have your guests stand too close, we do not want any accidents to happen.

Crêpes

2/3 CUP (90 G) ALL-PURPOSE FLOUR

2 TEASPOONS GRANULATED SUGAR

1/4 TEASPOON SALT

3 LARGE EGGS, LIGHTLY BEATEN

1 1/2 CUPS (375 ML) WHOLE MILK

1 TEASPOON PURE VANILLA EXTRACT

3 TABLESPOONS UNSALTED BUTTER, MELTED

1. In a medium mixing bowl, sift together the flour, sugar and salt. Make a well in the center. Pour the eggs into the well and stir from the center outward with a fork, as you would for fresh pasta. Add the milk and vanilla and stir until smooth and well blended. Cover with plastic wrap and chill in the refrigerator for at least 30 minutes.

2. Remove the crêpe batter from the refrigerator and let it come to room temperature. Stir in 1 tablespoon melted butter.

3. Place a 7-inch (17.5 cm) crêpe pan or nonstick omelet pan over medium heat. With a pastry brush, coat the pan with some of the remaining melted butter. With a small ladle, add a small amount of batter to the pan and swirl to coat the entire surface with a thin layer. When golden on the bottom (about 1 minute), flip the crêpe and cook for just a few seconds more. Transfer the crêpe to a plate and repeat with the remaining batter, brushing the pan with butter before cooking and stacking the crêpes as you go.

Sauce

2 TABLESPOONS GRANULATED SUGAR

1/2 STICK UNSALTED BUTTER

JUICE OF 2 ORANGES AND 1 LEMON

GRATED ZEST OF 1 ORANGE AND 1 LEMON

1/4 CUP (60 ML) GRAND MARNIER

1/4 CUP (60 ML) BRANDY

1. In a large sauté pan over medium heat, combine the sugar and half of the butter. Cook, stirring, until the sugar has turned light brown. Add the remaining butter and stir just until melted. Slowly add the orange juice and lemon juice and the grated orange and lemon zest.

2. Remove 12 crêpes from the stack (freeze any remaining crêpes, well wrapped, for another time). Fold them into fourths and add to the sauce. Heat through gently. Meanwhile, in a small saucepan, combine the Grand Marnier and brandy. While standing back, place the saucepan over medium heat and carefully tilt it slightly away from the body to ignite the alcohol. (If you do not have a gas stove, carefully ignite the mixture with a match held at the edge of the saucepan, tilting it slightly away from the body.) Move the saucepan back and forth constantly until the flames die out. Pour over the crêpes. Serve immediately on warm plates. Top with vanilla ice cream and whipped cream and…*voila!*

flourless chocolate cake

YIELD: 8 TO 10 SERVINGS

desserts

THIS RECIPE IS GREAT for chocohalics like myself!!! This is a decadent and rich tasting dessert that is so easy to make, yet uses only eight ingredients. Your guests will think you slaved over it for hours.

12 OUNCES (340 G) SEMISWEET CHOCOLATE CHIPS

1 TABLESPOON PURE VANILLA EXTRACT

1 TABLESPOON DARK RUM

1/4 CUP (60 ML) STRONG BREWED COFFEE

5 LARGE EGGS

1/2 CUP (70 G) GRANULATED SUGAR

3/4 CUP (200 ML) HEAVY CREAM

WHIPPED CREAM, FRESH FRUIT AND MINT LEAVES FOR GARNISH

1. Preheat the oven to 325°F/160°C. Coat a 10-inch (25 cm) springform cake pan with butter and wrap the outside of the pan with a double thickness of aluminum foil to prevent water from seeping in. Chill a large mixing bowl.

2. Place the chocolate, vanilla, rum and coffee in the top of a double boiler set over 1 inch (2.5 cm) of simmering (not boiling) water. Whisk until the chocolate is smooth and no small lumps remain. Turn off the heat and remove the mixture from the hot water. Transfer to a large bowl and let cool.

3. In a medium mixing bowl, combine the eggs and sugar. With an electric mixer, beat until pale in color, stopping 2 or 3 times to scrape down the sides of the bowl. Add 1/4 of the chocolate mixture and beat until incorporated. Pour this mixture into the remaining chocolate mixture. Stir until combined.

4. Bring a large kettle of water to a boil. Meanwhile, in the chilled mixing bowl, whip the cream until soft peaks form. With a rubber spatula, fold the whipped cream into the chocolate mixture until just combined. Pour the mixture into the prepared cake pan and cover the top with aluminum foil. Place in a roasting pan and pour enough boiling water into the roasting pan to come halfway up the outside of the cake pan. Bake for 30 minutes or until small cracks appear on the surface.

5. Remove the cake from the oven and let cool to room temperature in the pan on a wire rack. Chill in the refrigerator overnight until ready to serve.

6. To serve, unmold the cake and place on a chilled dessert plate. Garnish with whipped cream, fresh fruit and mint leaves.

key lime pie
with "never fall" meringue

VERY SIMPLY, a meringue is a mixture of stiffly beaten egg whites and granulated sugar. In order for sugar to dissolve completely, it must be beaten into the whites a tablespoon at a time. Meringues are placed into three categories: soft, hard or Italian. The soft type is used for pies, pudding and other desserts.

Filling

1¹/₂ CUPS (210 G) GRANULATED SUGAR

6 TABLESPOONS CORNSTARCH

1¹/₂ CUPS (375 ML) WATER

¹/₃ CUP (75 ML) FRESH LIME JUICE

3 LARGE EGG YOLKS

1¹/₂ TEASPOONS GRATED LIME ZEST

2 TEASPOONS WHITE VINEGAR

3 TABLESPOONS UNSALTED BUTTER

1 BAKED 9-INCH (22.5 CM) PIE SHELL

1. Combine the sugar and cornstarch in the top of a double boiler. Add the water and stir to combine. In a medium bowl, whisk the lime juice and egg yolks until well mixed; add to the cornstarch mixture and whisk until well blended.

2. Place the double boiler over 1 inch (2.5 cm) of boiling water and cook, stirring, until the mixture is thick and no starchy taste remains, about 25 minutes. Turn off the heat and remove the mixture from the hot water. Let cool slightly. Whisk in the grated lime zest, vinegar and butter until completely incorporated.

3. Pour the mixture into the pie shell, cover with plastic wrap and chill in the refrigerator until cold.

Meringue

1 TABLESPOON CORNSTARCH

2 TABLESPOONS COLD WATER

¹/₂ CUP (125 ML) BOILING WATER

3 LARGE EGG WHITES

6 TABLESPOONS GRANULATED SUGAR

1 TEASPOON PURE VANILLA EXTRACT

PINCH SALT

1. Preheat the oven to 350°F/ 180°C. In a small saucepan, combine the cornstarch and cold water; whisk until blended. Add the boiling water and place over medium heat. Cook, stirring, until the mixture is clear and thickened. Remove from the heat and let stand until completely cold.

2. In a large, grease-free mixing bowl, beat the egg whites with an electric mixer on medium speed until frothy. Increase the speed to high and gradually add the sugar, beating until the egg whites are stiff but not dry. Reduce the speed to low and add the vanilla and salt. Gradually beat in the cold cornstarch mixture. Increase the speed to high and beat until all the ingredients are fully incorporated.

3. Spread the meringue over the cooled pie filling and bake for 10 minutes, or until the top is lightly browned.

raspberry crème brûlée

desserts

YIELD: 6 SERVINGS

WE USUALLY THINK of burnt cream as the traditional French dish called crème brûlée. However, recipes for burnt cream appear in many old English cookbooks dating back to the eighteenth century. The caramel top was traditionally made using a "salamander"; a circular iron plate, heated to a high temperature and placed over the pudding to brown it. Today, I suggest placing it under the broiler until the sugar turns golden brown.

2 CUPS (500 ML) HEAVY CREAM

1 VANILLA BEAN, SPLIT

4 LARGE EGG YOLKS

1/2 CUP (70 G) GRANULATED SUGAR, PLUS MORE FOR SPRINKLING

1 1/2 CUPS (210 G) FRESH RASPBERRIES

1. Prepare a large bowl of ice water; set aside. Pour the cream into a medium saucepan. Use the tip of a blunt knife to scrape the vanilla bean seeds into the cream. Very slowly, bring the cream and vanilla to a boil over medium-low heat.

2. Meanwhile, bring about 1 inch (2.5 cm) of water to a simmer in a wide saucepan. Adjust the heat so that the water is at a bare simmer. In a large heatproof mixing bowl that can sit on the saucepan, combine the egg yolks and sugar. With an electric mixer, beat on high speed until pale in color, about 3 minutes, stopping 2 or 3 times to scrape down the sides of the bowl.

3. Set the bowl with the egg mixture over the simmering (not boiling) water and whisk constantly until the mixture is lemony looking, tripled in volume, and very thick. Keep the mixture over the simmering water as you whisk. (Take care that the eggs do not curdle. If necessary, momentarily remove the mixture from the heat if it gets too hot.)

4. When the cream boils, remove it and the egg mixture from the heat, continuing to whisk the egg mixture as it cools down slightly. Whisking constantly, slowly add the heavy cream to the egg mixture until completely blended. Strain the mixture through a fine sieve into a medium bowl. Place the bowl in the bowl of ice water to chill the mixture quickly. Cover with plastic wrap and refrigerate overnight before using.

5. To serve, divide the raspberries among six 4-ounce (60 ml) soufflé dishes or ramekins and spoon the crème brûlée mixture over them. Level the surface with a spatula and sprinkle some sugar over each dessert. Place the dishes under the broiler and heat until the crème brûlée mixture turns golden brown. (Alternatively, use a kitchen blowtorch to glaze the mixture.) Serve immediately.

raspberry tiramisu

TIRAMISÙ (which means "pick me up" in Italian) is a light composition of sponge cake or ladyfingers dipped in a coffee mixture, then layered with Mascarpone (an ultrarich Italian cream cheese) and grated chocolate. Although sometimes referred to as an Italian trifle, its texture is much lighter than that type of dessert.

1½ CUPS (210 G) MASCARPONE CHEESE

4 LARGE EGG YOLKS

½ CUP (70 G)
    PLUS 1 TABLESPOON
    GRANULATED SUGAR

½ CUP (125 ML) KAHLÚA LIQUEUR

½ CUP (125 ML) HEAVY CREAM

⅓ CUP (75 ML) STRONG BREWED COFFEE

1 CUP (250 ML) WHOLE MILK

36 LADYFINGER BISCUITS

1 CUP (140 G) FRESH RASPBERRIES

¼ CUP (35 G) COCOA POWDER

CHOCOLATE STICKS FOR GARNISH

RASPBERRY SAUCE, OPTIONAL

1. With a fork, stir the mascarpone until softened; reserve. Bring about 1 inch (2.5 cm) of water to a simmer in a wide saucepan. Adjust the heat so that the water is at a bare simmer.

2. In a large heatproof mixing bowl that can sit on the saucepan, combine the egg yolks and sugar. With an electric mixer, beat on high speed until pale in color, about 3 minutes, stopping 2 or 3 times to scrape down the sides of the bowl.

3. Set the bowl over the simmering (not boiling) water and whisk constantly until the mixture is lemony looking, tripled in volume, and very thick. Keep the mixture over the simmering water as you whisk. (Take care that the eggs do not curdle. If necessary, momentarily remove the mixture from the heat if it gets too hot.) Remove from the heat and whisk until cool.

4. Add the mascarpone and ¼ cup (60 ml) Kahlúa; whisk until well blended. In a chilled mixing bowl, whip the heavy cream until stiff but still glossy. Fold the whipped cream into the mascarpone mixture.

5. In a medium bowl, combine the remaining ¼ cup (60 ml) Kahlúa, the coffee and milk. Dip each ladyfinger biscuit in the liquid and use ⅓ of them to line an 8-inch oval (20 cm) dish, bottom and sides. Spread ⅓ of the mascarpone mixture over the biscuits and top with another third of the biscuits; press down lightly. Layer another ⅓ of the mascarpone mixture on top and sprinkle with the raspberries, letting them sink in. Top with the remaining biscuits and mascarpone mixture.

6. Cover with plastic wrap and chill in the refrigerator for 2 hours, until set. Place the cocoa powder in a medium sieve and sprinkle it over the top. Garnish with chocolate sticks. Cut into wedges and serve with raspberry sauce, if desired.

vanilla soufflé

desserts

A SOUFFLÉ IS A LIGHT, airy mixture that usually begins with a thick egg yolk-based sauce or purée that is lightened by stiffly beaten egg whites. Dessert soufflés may be baked, chilled or frozen and are most often flavored with fruit purees, chocolate, lemon or liqueurs. Soufflés are customarily baked in a classic soufflé dish, which is round and has straight sides to facilitate the soufflé's rising. Foil or parchment "collars" are sometimes wrapped around the outside of a soufflé dish so that the top of the foil or paper rises about 2 inches (5 cm) above the rim of the dish.

1 CUP (250 ML) WHOLE MILK

1/2 CUP (70 G) GRANULATED SUGAR

2 TABLESPOONS UNSALTED BUTTER

2 VANILLA BEANS, SPLIT

1 TABLESPOON ALL-PURPOSE FLOUR

4 LARGE EGGS, SEPARATED

1. Preheat the oven to 375°F/200°C. Generously butter six 6-ounce (200 ml) soufflé dishes or ramekins. Dust the dishes with a little sugar; tilt to coat and tap out the excess. Set aside.

2. In a medium heavy saucepan, combine the milk, 1/4 cup (35 g) sugar, and the butter over medium heat. Bring to a boil. Reduce the heat to low and use the tip of a blunt knife to scrape the vanilla bean seeds into the mixture. Gently simmer, stirring occasionally, until the vanilla has infused the mixture, about 15 minutes.

3. Add the flour and cook, stirring constantly, until the mixture leaves the sides of the saucepan clean, about 2 minutes. Remove from the heat and let cool. Transfer the mixture to a large bowl.

4. One by one, add the egg yolks to the milk mixture, beating well after each addition. (The mixture may be made ahead to this point, covered and refrigerated for up to 1 day. Bring to room temperature before proceeding.)

5. In a large, grease-free mixing bowl, beat the egg whites with an electric mixer on medium speed until frothy. Increase the speed to high and gradually add the remaining 1/4 cup (35 g) sugar, beating until the egg whites form soft peaks.

6. Spoon one-third of the egg whites into the milk mixture and gently mix until the batter is lightened somewhat. With a rubber spatula, fold in the remaining egg whites, taking care not to deflate them.

7. Bring a large kettle of water to a boil. Line a roasting pan with a folded kitchen towel. Place the prepared soufflé dishes in the roasting pan and fill them three-fourths full with the soufflé mixture. Pour enough boiling water into the roasting pan to come one-third up the sides of the dishes. Bake for 20 minutes, or until doubled in height and golden. Remove the dishes from the water bath and serve immediately with raspberry sauce or chocolate sauce.

ship shape

HERE'S A THOUGHT. Fabulous foods do not always have to be fattening!! It's easy to make food taste good by using cream and butter or by covering it with a heavy sauce. What's harder is to make things taste great in a healthful, low-fat way. ⚓ WE NOW KNOW that the right way to eat is to enjoy a healthy balanced diet with an emphasis on fruits, vegetables and grains. At Royal Caribbean, we are working to continually update and upgrade our already vast repertoire of dishes designed to reflect the new, healthier lifestyles. I've chosen some of our all-time favorites and adapted the recipes for you to make at home. These are not "diet" dishes; they're foods designed to help you maintain a healthy lifestyle, without feeling deprived. 👑 FOR MANY PEOPLE, eating light means eating fish. So how does Grilled Mahi Mahi with Pineapple Curry Sauce sound? Feel more like a salad? Crunchy Chicken Salad with Granny Smith Apples and Bulgur makes a delicious, nutritious meal—with lots of crunch. All of the dishes in this section are perfect to fuel your hungry family, and are lovely enough for a dinner party. Everyone will thank you for making good food with great health in mind.

NORDIC EMPRESS

carrot-ginger soup

GINGER, a plant from tropical and subtropical regions, has a tanned skin and a flesh that ranges in color from pale yellow to ivory. The flavor is peppery and slightly sweet, while the aroma is pungent and spicy. This extremely versatile root has long been a mainstay in Asian and Indian cooking and has since found its way into American and European cooking. Fresh ginger is found in two forms—young and mature. Young ginger has a pale skin that requires no peeling. It also has a much milder flavor than mature ginger. Mature ginger has a smoother surface and has a fresh, spicy fragrance. Fresh unpeeled ginger can be stored, refrigerated and tightly wrapped for up to 3 weeks. It may also be frozen for up to 3 months.

1 TEASPOON EXTRA-VIRGIN OLIVE OIL

1 SMALL ONION, CHOPPED

1 STALK CELERY, CHOPPED

1 TABLESPOON MINCED FRESH GINGER

1 POUND (454 G) CARROTS, THINLY SLICED

4 1/2 CUPS (1.1 L) VEGETABLE STOCK,
    PLUS EXTRA AS NEEDED (SEE PAGE 153)

1 BAY LEAF

KOSHER SALT TO TASTE

3 TABLESPOONS CHOPPED FRESH ITALIAN PARSLEY

1/2 CUP (70 G) COOKED WHITE RICE, KEPT HOT (OPTIONAL)

4 SPRIGS PARSLEY FOR GARNISH

1. Heat the oil in a soup pot over medium heat. Add the onion and celery and cook, stirring, until the vegetables soften and become translucent (do not let the vegetables brown). Add the ginger and cook, stirring, for 1 minute more.

2. Add the carrots, vegetable stock and bay leaf. Season with kosher salt and bring to boil. Reduce the heat to low and cook, partially covered, until the carrots are fork-tender, about 35 to 40 minutes. Remove from the heat, remove and discard the bay leaf, and let cool for 10 minutes.

3. Transfer the contents of the pot in batches to a food processor or blender. Purée until smooth. Return the soup to the pot and bring it to a gentle simmer. Add more stock as necessary if the soup is too thick. Adjust the seasoning and stir in the chopped parsley.

4. Divide the rice, if using, among 4 warmed soup bowls and ladle the soup over it. Garnish each bowl with a sprig of parsley and serve immediately.

watermelon gazpacho

ship shape

⚓

NATIVE TO AFRICA, the watermelon is one of two broad categories of melon, the other being the muskmelon. Although there are many varieties, the most popular is the large, elongated, oval shape with a variegated or striped, two-tone green or gray-green rind. Most average between 15 to 35 pounds (6.8-16 kg). Watermelons are available from May to September with their peak being from mid-June to late August. Avoid melons that have soft spots, gashes or other blemishes on the rind. They should be stored whole, in the refrigerator if possible (if not in a cool dark place) for no more than a week. Cut watermelons should be tightly wrapped and used within a day or so.

1 CUP PEELED, SEEDED AND THINLY SLICED CUCUMBER

1/4 TEASPOON KOSHER SALT

6 CUPS (840 G) CUBED SEEDLESS WATERMELON

1/2 CUP (125 ML) CRANBERRY JUICE COCKTAIL

1 RED BELL PEPPER, CORED, SEEDED AND FINELY CHOPPED

1 MEDIUM RED ONION, FINELY CHOPPED

1 STALK CELERY, FINELY CHOPPED

1/4 CUP (35 G) MINCED FRESH ITALIAN PARSLEY

2 TO 3 TABLESPOONS FRESH LIME JUICE

1 TABLESPOON SHERRY VINEGAR

8 FRESH MINT LEAVES FOR GARNISH

1. In a small bowl, toss the cucumber with the salt and set aside.

2. In a food processor or blender, combine the watermelon and cranberry juice. Pulse briefly until just blended (do not over process or the juice will become frothy and pale.) Strain the mixture through a fine sieve over a nonreactive bowl, pushing down on the solids to extract as much of the liquid as you can, leaving the pulp behind.

3. Stir in the bell pepper, onion, celery, parsley, lime juice and vinegar. Cover and refrigerate for 1 hour to let the flavors blend.

4. To serve, rinse the cucumber and pat dry with paper towels. Divide the soup among chilled soup bowls and garnish with the cucumber and mint leaves.

crunchy chicken salad
with granny smith apples and bulgur

YIELD: 4 SERVINGS

BULGUR is a nutritious staple in the Middle East, it consists of wheat kernels that have been steamed, dried and crushed. Often confused with cracked wheat, it is not the same. Bulgur has a tender, chewy texture and comes in coarse, medium and fine grains.

Tofu, also known as soybean curd or bean curd, is made from curdled soymilk, which is an iron-rich liquid extracted from ground, cooked soybeans. These are drained and pressed in a process similar to cheesemaking and the result is tofu. Popular through much of Asia, it has a mild, nutty flavor that gives it a chameleon-like capability to take on the flavor of the food with which it cooks. Available in Asian markets, health-food stores and supermarkets, it is sold in a variety of forms with the most popular form being packed in water. Tofu is very perishable and should be refrigerated for no more than a week or frozen for up to 3 months. Tofu is easy to digest, low in calories, high in calcium, sodium, protein and is cholesterol free.

Tofu Mayonnaise
YIELD: 1^2/$_3$ CUPS (700 ML)

1 TABLESPOON MINCED SHALLOT

1 TABLESPOON DIJON MUSTARD

2^1/$_2$ TABLESPOONS APPLE CIDER VINEGAR

10 OUNCES (300 G) SOFT TOFU

1 TEASPOON FRESHLY GROUND BLACK PEPPER

1/4 CUP (60 ML) WATER

SALT AND FRESHLY GROUND PEPPER TO TASTE

In a food processor, purée all the ingredients until smooth. Season to taste with salt and pepper. Transfer to a container and refrigerate until ready to use.

Chicken Salad
1/4 CUP (35 G) FINE OR MEDIUM-GRAIN BULGUR

1 POUND (454 G) BONELESS, SKINLESS CHICKEN BREASTS

1 TEASPOON EXTRA-VIRGIN OLIVE OIL

1/4 TEASPOON DRIED TARRAGON

1/4 TEASPOON FRESHLY GROUND BLACK PEPPER

1 LARGE GRANNY SMITH APPLE, PEELED, CORED AND DICED

1 TABLESPOON FRESH LIME JUICE

1 CUP (140 G) DICED CELERY

1/4 CUP (35 G) CHOPPED FRESH ITALIAN PARSLEY

2 TEASPOONS CHOPPED FRESH TARRAGON

1/2 CUP (60 ML) TOFU MAYONNAISE (RECIPE ABOVE)

1/4 POUND (112 G) MIXED BABY LETTUCES OR MESCLUN GREENS, WASHED AND DRIED

1 TABLESPOON CHOPPED FRESH MINT

1. Place the bulgur in a medium bowl. Add 1/2 cup (60 ml) boiling water and stir to combine. Let stand until swollen and tender but still a little crunchy; about 30 minutes.

2. Meanwhile, preheat the oven to 350°F/180°C. Heat a charcoal or gas grill to medium. Lightly coat a baking sheet and the grill top with vegetable oil spray.

3. Rub the chicken breasts with the oil, tarragon and pepper. Grill on both sides only until well marked, about 2 to 3 minutes on each side. Transfer to the prepared baking sheet and bake, uncovered, for 8 to 10 minutes in the oven, until the juices run clear when the meat is pierced with a fork. Remove from the oven, let cool, and cut into 1/2-inch (1.25 cm) cubes. Transfer to a large nonreactive bowl.

4. Add the apple to the chicken and drizzle with the lime juice. Add the celery, parsley and tarragon and toss until well combined. Add the tofu mayonnaise and toss gently to coat.

5. To serve, line 4 chilled plates with the lettuces or mesclun. Spoon the chicken salad on the greens. Stir the mint into the reserved bulgur and sprinkle it over the salad. Serve immediately.

ship shape caesar salad

YIELD: 4 TO 6 SERVINGS

THIS IS THE LOW-FAT version of the Traditional Caesar Salad found found on page 50.

4 SLICES SOURDOUGH BREAD CUT INTO CUBES

4 TABLESPOONS EXTRA-VIRGIN OLIVE OIL

1 TABLESPOON PREPARED OR BASIC MAYONNAISE (PAGE 53)

1 TABLESPOON FRESH LEMON JUICE

1/2 TEASPOON DIJON MUSTARD

1/4 TEASPOON WORCESTERSHIRE SAUCE

1 CLOVE GARLIC, MINCED

2 TABLESPOONS GRATED PARMESAN CHEESE

3 HEARTS ROMAINE LETTUCE, WASHED AND DRIED

SHAVED PARMESAN FOR GARNISH

FRESHLY GROUND PEPPER TO TASTE

1. Preheat the oven to 350°F/180°C. In a bowl, combine the bread cubes and 1 tablespoon oil; toss to coat. Transfer to a baking sheet and bake for 10 minutes, or until golden brown. Transfer to a plate lined with paper towels to drain. Reserve.

2. In a nonreactive bowl, combine the remaining 3 tablespoons oil, mayonnaise, lemon juice, mustard, Worcestershire sauce, garlic and Parmesan. Stir until well blended.

3. Remove any wilted outer leaves from the romaine and slice in half lengthwise. Divide the romaine among chilled plates and top with the croutons. Drizzle with the dressing and garnish with shaved Parmesan. Sprinkle with pepper and serve immediately.

grilled tuna niçoise

Note: Any type of fish such as salmon or broiled cod (*shown in photo, left*) may be substituted for the tuna.

Roasted Tomato-Basil Dressing

1 MEDIUM TOMATO, CORED

1 TEASPOON FINELY CHOPPED SHALLOT

1/4 TEASPOON MINCED GARLIC

1 TABLESPOON WATER

2 TEASPOONS BALSAMIC VINEGAR

1/8 TEASPOON FRESHLY GROUND BLACK PEPPER

1 TABLESPOON CHIFFONADE OF FRESH BASIL (SEE BASIC KNIFE TECHNIQUES, P. 12)

SALT AND FRESHLY GROUND PEPPER TO TASTE

1. Heat a covered charcoal or gas grill to medium hot. Grill the tomato, turning often, until the skin begins to blister. Remove, let cool and cut into quarters.

2. In a blender or food processor, combine the tomato, shallot, garlic, water, vinegar and pepper. Process until the tomato is coarsely puréed. Add the basil and pulse to combine. Season to taste with salt and pepper. Transfer to a container and refrigerate until ready to use.

Potato and Vegetable Mixture

1 POUND (454 G) RED POTATOES, HALVED OR QUARTERED

1 RED PEPPER CUT INTO STRIPS

12 BLACK OLIVES CURED IN BRINE, HALVED

1 SMALL YELLOW ONION JULIENNE

2 TABLESPOONS RED WINE VINEGAR

1 TABLESPOON EXTRA-VIRGIN OLIVE OIL

SALT AND FRESHLY GROUND PEPPER TO TASTE

1. Cook the potatoes in a large saucepan of boiling water just until fork-tender, about 15 minutes. Drain and let cool. Slice into 1/4-inch (6 mm) slices.

2. In a large nonreactive bowl, whisk the oil and vinegar. Add the potatoes, red peppers, black olives and onions. Season with salt and pepper and set aside.

To Assemble

VEGETABLE OIL SPRAY

4 4-OUNCE (114 G) TUNA STEAKS, ABOUT 1/2-INCH (1.25 CM) THICK

1 TEASPOON EXTRA-VIRGIN OLIVE OIL

1 TEASPOON FRESHLY GROUND BLACK PEPPER

1/4 POUND (112 G) GREEN BEANS

4 LARGE LETTUCE LEAVES, SUCH AS BIBB OR BOSTON, WASHED AND DRIED

2 MEDIUM TOMATOES, CORED AND QUARTERED

1. Heat a covered charcoal or gas grill to medium hot and spray the grill with vegetable oil spray. Brush the tuna on both sides with the oil and season with the pepper. Grill the tuna until marked, about 3 minutes on each side. Remove from the heat.

2. Prepare a bowl of ice water. Bring a medium saucepan of salted water to a boil. Add the green beans and cook just until bright green and tender-crisp, about 5 minutes. Remove the beans with a strainer and shock them in the ice water to stop the cooking. Drain and set aside.

3. To serve, line 4 chilled plates with the lettuce. Garnish the plates with the green beans, potato and vegetable mixture and tomatoes. Top with the tuna and serve with the roasted tomato-basil dressing on the side.

baked halibut
on savoy cabbage

YIELD: 4 SERVINGS

SAVOY CABBAGE has a loose, full head with crinkled leaves and a mild flavor. It is bright green, crisp and sweet and is ideal with fish. When choosing this type of cabbage, make sure that the leaves are fresh and taut, with no sign of browning. It should be refrigerated tightly for no more than a week.

1 TEASPOON EXTRA-VIRGIN OLIVE OIL

1/2 CUP (70 G) THINLY SLICED RED ONION

4 4-OUNCE (114 G) HALIBUT STEAKS

1/2 CUP (125 ML) DRY WHITE WINE OR FISH STOCK (SEE PAGE 154)

1/4 TEASPOON FRESHLY GROUND BLACK PEPPER

4 SPRIGS LEMON THYME OR 1/2 TEASPOON DRIED LEMON THYME

8 SAVOY CABBAGE LEAVES

1/2 CUP (113 G) PLAIN NONFAT YOGURT

2 TEASPOONS PREPARED HORSERADISH

1 LEMON, QUARTERED

1. In a large nonstick pan with a lid, heat the oil over medium heat. Add the onion and cook, stirring, until softened and translucent, 4 to 5 minutes.

2. Lay the halibut steaks in a single layer over the onion and add the wine or fish stock. Season with the pepper and lemon thyme. Cover tightly and cook until the fish is opaque and heated through, about 15 minutes.

3. Meanwhile, place the cabbage leaves in the top of a steamer set over 1 inch (2.5 cm) of boiling water. Cover and steam until the leaves soften but are still a vivid green, 8 to 10 minutes.

4. To serve, arrange 2 cabbage leaves on each plate. Center the halibut and onion over them and ladle some of the cooking liquid over the halibut. In a small bowl, combine the yogurt and horse-radish. Spoon a dollop of the horseradish sauce onto each piece of halibut, garnish with a lemon wedge and serve immediately.

Note: A good substitute for halibut is salmon.

stir-fried chicken
with ginger sauce and steamed vegetables

2 BONELESS, SKINLESS CHICKEN
BREASTS

1 TEASPOON MINCED FRESH
GINGER

1/2 TEASPOON DARK ASIAN
SESAME OIL

2 TEASPOONS LOW-SODIUM
SOY SAUCE

1 TABLESPOON FRESH LIME JUICE

1 TABLESPOON SZECHUAN
PEPPERCORNS, CRACKED
(SEE NOTE BELOW)

2 TEASPOONS CANOLA OIL

1/2 RED BELL PEPPER, CORED,
SEEDED, AND CUT INTO
1/4-INCH (6 MM) STRIPS

5 SHIITAKE MUSHROOMS,
STEMMED, WIPED CLEAN AND
THINLY SLICED

1/4 CUP (60 ML) VEGETABLE
STOCK (SEE PAGE 153)
OR WATER

1 CUP (140 G) BROCCOLI
FLORETS

1/4 POUND (112 G) SNOW PEAS

1/4 POUND (112 G) BABY
CARROTS

1 1/2 CUPS (210 G) BROWN RICE,
COOKED AND KEPT HOT

1/4 CUP (35 G) CHOPPED FRESH
CILANTRO LEAVES

1. Cut the chicken into ³/4-inch (2 cm) pieces and place in a large nonreactive bowl. Add the ginger, sesame oil, soy sauce, lime juice and peppercorns. Toss to coat. Cover and refrigerate for at least 1 hour but no longer than 8 hours.

2. In a large heavy saucepan or wok, heat the canola oil over medium-high heat. Add the chicken with its marinade and cook, stirring, for 3 to 4 minutes. The chicken will be slightly underdone.

3. Add the bell pepper and mushrooms and cook, stirring, for 2 to 3 minutes more. Add the vegetable stock and scrape up any browned bits from the bottom of the pan.

4. Meanwhile, combine the broccoli, snow peas and carrots in the top of a steamer set over 1 inch (2.5 cm) of boiling water. Cover and steam the vegetables just until they are fork-tender.

5. To serve, divide the rice among 4 warmed plates. Spoon the chicken and stir-fried vegetables along with any sauce over the rice. Garnish with the steamed vegetables and cilantro and serve immediately.

Note: Thai or Vietnamese chili paste may be used instead of the peppercorns.

oatmeal cookies

YIELD: 36 COOKIES

OATS are by far the most nutritious of the cereal grains once they have been cleaned, toasted, hulled and cleaned again. Found in health food stores and supermarkets, they are high in vitamins B-1, B-2, E and are high in soluble fiber, which is a leading contender in the fight against high cholesterol.

VEGETABLE OIL SPRAY

2 LARGE EGGS, AT ROOM TEMPERATURE

3 LARGE EGG WHITES, AT ROOM TEMPERATURE

1 TEASPOON PURE VANILLA EXTRACT

1 TEASPOON GROUND CINNAMON

1/2 TEASPOON SALT

1 TEASPOON BAKING POWDER

1/2 CUP (70 G) GRANULATED SUGAR

1/4 CUP (35 G) PACKED LIGHT BROWN SUGAR

2 3/4 CUPS (380 G) ROLLED OATS

1/3 CUP (50 G) WHOLE WHEAT FLOUR

1. Preheat the oven to 350°F/180°C. Lightly coat 2 baking sheets with vegetable oil spray.

2. In a mixing bowl, combine the eggs, egg whites, vanilla, cinnamon, salt, baking powder and both sugars. With an electric mixer, beat on high speed, stopping 2 or 3 times to scrape down the sides of the bowl, until the mixture is doubled in volume and forms a ribbon when the beaters are raised. With a rubber spatula, fold in the oats and flour.

3. Drop rounded tablespoons of the dough 1 inch (2.5 cm) apart onto the prepared baking sheets. Bake in batches for 15 to 20 minutes, or until lightly browned. Remove the cookies immediately from the baking sheets and let cool on a wire rack.

sauces

Understanding Sauces A sauce may be defined as a flavorful liquid, usually thickened, which is used to season, flavor and enhance other foods. A sauce adds many enticing qualities to foods, such as moistness, flavor, richness, appearance (color and shine), interest and appetite appeal.

The Structure of Sauces There are three major components that make a sauce: a liquid (the body of the sauce), a thickening agent and additional seasonings and flavoring ingredients.

LIQUID: A liquid ingredient provides the body or base for most sauces, for example:

White stock (chicken, veal, or fish) for *velouté* sauces

Brown stock (beef, veal and chicken) for brown sauce *(espagnole)*

Clarified butter for hollandaise and *Béarnaise*

THICKENING AGENTS: A sauce must be thick enough to cling lightly to the food. Otherwise, it will run off the food and lie like a puddle on the plate. Starches are the most common thickening agents, but there are others as well. Flour is the principal starch used in sauce making.

Roux is the most commonly used thickener. It is a cooked mixture of equal parts by weight of fat and flour. Clarified butter is preferred for the finest sauces because of its flavor.

TO MAKE CLARIFIED BUTTER, cut unsalted butter into small pieces and melt over moderate heat in a small saucepan. When melted, skim off the foam, remove the pan from the heat, and let stand for a few minutes to allow the milk solids to settle. Skim off the clear yellow liquid—the clarified butter—and leave the milky residue on the bottom of the pan.

BASIC PROCEDURE FOR MAKING ALL ROUX:

1. Melt the fat.

2. Add the correct amount of flour and stir until the fat and flour are thoroughly mixed.

3. Cook to the required degree for blond or brown roux. (Blonde roux is cooked only until it begins to change to a slightly darker color. Cooking must then be stopped. Blonde roux is used for *velouté* sauces, which are based on white stocks and are pale ivory in color. Brown roux is cooked until it takes on a light brown color and nutty aroma. Cooking must take place over low heat so the roux browns easily without scorching.)

Butter Sauces

Hollandaise and Béarnaise are the two most elegant butter sauces in French cuisine. One is essentially a variation of the other: Béarnaise is a type of hollandaise sauce with the addition of chopped fresh tarragon leaves and chervil.

béarnaise sauce

YIELD: 2 CUPS (500 ML)

3 STICKS (360 G) UNSALTED BUTTER
2 SHALLOTS, FINELY CHOPPED
6 TABLESPOONS WHITE WINE VINEGAR
2 TABLESPOONS CHOPPED FRESH TARRAGON LEAVES
6 LARGE EGG YOLKS
2 TABLESPOONS FRESH LEMON JUICE
SALT AND FRESHLY GROUND BLACK PEPPER TO TASTE
CAYENNE PEPPER TO TASTE
2 TABLESPOONS CHOPPED FRESH CHERVIL

1. Clarify the butter: Melt the butter in a medium saucepan over low heat. Cook until the butterfat becomes clear and the milk solids drop to the bottom of the pan. Skim the surface foam as the butter separates. Carefully spoon the clear butterfat into a second saucepan and keep warm. Discard the milky liquid at the bottom of the first saucepan.

2. In a small nonreactive saucepan, combine the shallots, vinegar and tarragon over medium heat. Simmer until the liquid is reduced to 1 tablespoon. Strain and discard the solids.

3. Transfer the shallot liquid to the top of a double-boiler set over 1 inch (2.5 cm) of simmering (not boiling) water. A clean side towel may be used to keep the bowl steady. Add the egg yolks and lemon juice and season with salt, pepper and cayenne. Gently cook, whisking constantly, until the eggs become foamy. (Do not let the sauce come to a boil.)

4. Slowly drizzle in the warm clarified butter, whisking constantly, until the sauce is thickened. Turn off the heat and remove the mixture from the hot water. Strain through a fine sieve into a clean double-boiler or a warmed bowl. Adjust the seasonings and stir in the chopped chervil. Warm water may be used to thin the sauce out to the desired consistency. Keep warm or serve immediately.

hollandaise sauce

sauces

YIELD: ABOUT 2 CUPS (500 ML)

1 POUND (454 G) UNSALTED
BUTTER

4 TABLESPOONS FINELY CHOPPED
SHALLOTS

6 TABLESPOONS WHITE WINE
VINEGAR

16 BLACK PEPPERCORNS,
CRUSHED

6 LARGE EGG YOLKS

2 TABLESPOONS FRESH
LEMON JUICE

SALT TO TASTE

TABASCO HOT PEPPER SAUCE OR
CAYENNE PEPPER TO TASTE

1. Clarify the butter: Melt the butter in a medium saucepan over low heat. Cook until the butterfat becomes clear and the milk solids drop to the bottom of the pan. Skim the surface foam as the butter separates. Carefully spoon the clear butterfat into a second saucepan and keep warm. Discard the milky liquid at the bottom of the first saucepan.

2. In a small nonreactive saucepan, combine the shallots, vinegar and peppercorns over medium heat. Cook, stirring, for 2 to 3 minutes. Strain and discard the solids.

3. Transfer the shallot liquid to the top of a double-boiler set over 1 inch (2.5 cm) of simmering (not boiling) water. A clean side towel may be used in between the bowl and simmering water. Add the egg yolks and gently cook, whisking constantly, until the eggs become thick and frothy. (Do not let the sauce come to a boil.) The mixture should become pale in color. Blend in the lemon juice and season with salt and Tabasco or cayenne pepper.

4. Turn off the heat and remove the mixture from the hot water. Slowly drizzle in the warm clarified butter, whisking constantly, until the sauce thickens into the consistency of heavy cream. Strain through a fine sieve into a clean double-boiler or a warmed bowl and adjust the seasonings. A little warm water may be added to thin the sauce out to the desired consistency. Keep warm or serve immediately.

White Sauces

White sauces are typically used for chicken or fish and seafood dishes. Below are recipes for four of the most common white sauces: Chicken Velouté Sauce, Sauce Suprême, Fish Velouté Sauce and White Wine Sauce.

chicken velouté sauce

YIELD: 2 CUPS (500 ML)

4 TABLESPOONS UNSALTED BUTTER
1/4 CUP (35 G) ALL-PURPOSE FLOUR
2 CUPS (500 ML) CHICKEN STOCK (SEE PAGE 152)
SALT AND CAYENNE PEPPER TO TASTE

1. Clarify the butter: Melt the butter in a small saucepan over low heat. Cook until the butterfat becomes clear and the milk solids drop to the bottom of the pan. Skim the surface foam as the butter separates. Carefully spoon the clear butterfat into a bowl and set aside. Discard the milky liquid at the bottom of the saucepan.

2. Make the roux: In a medium saucepan, melt 2 tablespoons clarified butter over medium heat. Whisk in the flour and cook, stirring, for 2 minutes (do not let the mixture darken in color). Remove the roux from the heat and let cool.

3. Make the velouté: In another medium saucepan, bring the chicken stock to a boil over medium-high heat. Pour the stock into the pan with the roux and whisk until well blended. Return the saucepan to the heat and cook, stirring, over medium-high heat until the mixture boils. Reduce the heat to low and simmer, stirring constantly, for 30 minutes. Season with salt and cayenne pepper.

4. Remove from the heat and strain through a fine sieve into a double-boiler or warmed bowl. Keep warm or serve immediately.

sauce suprême

³/₄ cup (200 ml) chicken stock (see page 152)

1¹/₂ cups (375 ml) chicken velouté sauce (see page 146)

¹/₂ cup (125 ml) heavy cream

Salt and cayenne pepper to taste

Fresh lemon juice to taste

1. In a small nonstick saucepan, slowly simmer the chicken stock over medium-low heat until reduced by three-fourths (do not let the stock turn brown).

2. Meanwhile, in a medium saucepan, simmer the chicken velouté over medium heat. Add the heavy cream and simmer, stirring, for 2 minutes.

3. Whisk the reduced stock into the velouté mixture and cook, stirring, until the sauce coats the back of a spoon. Strain through a fine sieve into a double-boiler or warmed bowl. Season with salt, cayenne and lemon juice. Keep warm or serve immediately.

white wine sauce

YIELD: 2 CUPS (500 ML)

1 tablespoon finely chopped shallot

1 tablespoon chopped parsley stems

¹/₂ cup (125 ml) dry white wine

2 cups (500 ml) fish velouté sauce (see page 148)

Salt and freshly ground white pepper to taste

1. In a small nonreactive saucepan, combine the shallot, parsley stems and wine over medium heat. Simmer until the liquid is reduced by half.

2. Meanwhile, in a medium saucepan, simmer the fish velouté over medium heat. Add the reduced wine mixture and bring to a boil. Reduce the heat and simmer, stirring, until the sauce coats the back of a spoon.

3. Strain through a fine sieve lined with cheesecloth into a double-boiler or warmed bowl. Season with salt and pepper. Keep warm or serve immediately.

fish velouté sauce

s a u c e s

YIELD: 2 CUPS (500 ML)

4 TABLESPOONS UNSALTED
  BUTTER

1/4 CUP (35 G) ALL-PURPOSE
  FLOUR

2 CUPS (500 ML) FISH STOCK
  (SEE PAGE 154)

SALT AND CAYENNE PEPPER
  TO TASTE

1. Clarify the butter: Melt the butter in a small saucepan over low heat. Cook until the butterfat becomes clear and the milk solids drop to the bottom of the pan. Skim the surface foam as the butter separates. Carefully spoon the clear butterfat into a bowl and set aside. Discard the milky liquid at the bottom of the saucepan.

2. Make the roux: In a medium saucepan, melt 2 tablespoons clarified butter over medium heat. Whisk in the flour and cook, stirring, for 2 minutes (do not let the mixture darken in color). Remove the roux from the heat and let cool.

3. Make the velouté: In another medium saucepan, bring the fish stock to a boil over medium-high heat. Pour the stock into the pan with the roux and whisk until well blended. Return the saucepan to the heat and cook, stirring, over medium-high heat until the mixture boils. Reduce the heat to low and simmer, stirring constantly, for 30 minutes. Season with salt and cayenne pepper.

4. Remove from the heat and strain through a fine sieve into a double-boiler or warmed bowl. Keep warm or serve immediately.

Brown Sauces

Full flavored and rich, brown sauces and their variations are typically served with beef, pork, lamb and game.

demi-glace

YIELD: 2 CUPS (500 ML)

2 CUPS (500 ML) BROWN SAUCE
(SEE RECIPE RIGHT)

2 CUPS (500 ML) BEEF STOCK
(SEE PAGE 151) OR DARK CHICKEN
STOCK (SEE PAGE 152)

SALT AND FRESHLY GROUND
BLACK PEPPER TO TASTE

In a medium saucepan, combine the brown sauce and beef stock over medium heat. Simmer until the liquid is reduced by half. Strain through a fine sieve lined with cheesecloth into a double boiler or warmed bowl. Season with salt and pepper. Keep warm or serve immediately.

brown sauce (espagnole)

YIELD: 2 CUPS (500 ML)

4 TABLESPOONS UNSALTED BUTTER

3/4 CUP (100 G) DICED ONION

1/3 CUP (50 G) DICED CARROT

1/2 CUP (70 G) DICED CELERY

1/2 CUP (70 G) ALL-PURPOSE FLOUR

5 CUPS (1.25 L) BEEF STOCK (SEE PAGE 151) OR DARK CHICKEN STOCK (PAGE 152)

3 TABLESPOONS CANNED TOMATO PUREE

1 BOUQUET GARNI (1/2 BAY LEAF, 1/4 TEASPOON CHOPPED FRESH THYME, AND 4 TO 6 PARSLEY STEMS BUNDLED IN A PIECE OF CHEESECLOTH AND TIED WITH STRING)

SALT AND FRESHLY GROUND BLACK PEPPER TO TASTE

1. In a medium saucepan, heat the butter over medium-high heat. Add the onion, carrot and celery and cook, stirring, until the vegetables turn golden brown, about 20 minutes. Reduce the heat to low and whisk in the flour. Cook, stirring, until the flour turns light brown and acquires a nutty aroma.

2. Gradually whisk in the stock and tomato purée and increase the heat to medium-high. Cook, stirring constantly, until the mixture comes to a boil. Reduce the heat to low and bring to a simmer. With a small ladle or slotted spoon, skim the surface.

3. Add the bouquet garni and simmer until the sauce is reduced by half, skimming as necessary. Strain through a fine sieve lined with cheesecloth into a double-boiler or warmed bowl. Season with salt and pepper. Keep warm or serve immediately.

stocks

STOCKS ARE FLAVORFUL liquids produced by simmering bones, meat trimmings, vegetables and other aromatic ingredients in water. Stocks are further categorized into either white or brown stocks. Each of which are the basis for soups, stews and sauces.

White Stock

THESE ARE MADE FROM meaty bones and trimmings from veal, poultry and some types of game and fish. The bones are most often blanched in order to remove any impurities that might cloud or discolor the finished stock. White beef stock, also known as a "neutral stock" is often used in vegetable soups or bean dishes. White stock can contribute a significant body to these dishes, while still allowing the flavor of the major ingredient to dominate the dish being served.

SOVEREIGN OF THE SEAS

Brown Stock

BROWN STOCKS are prepared first by cooking meaty bones and meat trimmings to a deep brown color. Mirepoix (onions, celery and carrots) and tomatoes are added as well, before they are simmered. This changes both the flavor and color of the finished stock. Brown stocks are most valuable in sauce cookery. They are the foundation for brown sauce, jus lié, demi-glace and pan gravies.

beef stock

4 POUNDS (1.8 KG) BEEF BONES

2 MEDIUM ONIONS, SKIN
LEFT ON, CUT INTO CHUNKS

1 POUND (454 G)
VEAL TRIMMINGS

2 CARROTS, CUT INTO 1/2-INCH
(1.25 CM) CHUNKS

2 STALKS CELERY, CUT INTO
1/2-INCH (1.25 CM) CHUNKS

2 MEDIUM TOMATOES,
CUT INTO CHUNKS

1 LEEK, WHITE AND LIGHT
GREEN PARTS ONLY, WASHED
AND CUT INTO 1/2-INCH
(1.25 CM) CHUNKS

3 SPRIGS PARSLEY, WITH STEMS

3 SPRIGS THYME

1 LARGE BAY LEAF

6 WHOLE BLACK PEPPERCORNS

1. Preheat the oven to 400°F/200°C. Arrange the beef bones and onions in a single layer in a large roasting pan. Scatter the veal trimmings around the bones. Roast, uncovered, for 1 hour, or until the bones are golden brown on all sides. Transfer the bones to a large stockpot.

2. Add the remaining ingredients to the bones in the stockpot and pour in enough cold water to cover by 2 inches (5 cm). Bring to a boil, uncovered, over medium-high heat. Reduce the heat to very low and simmer very gently, with just a few bubbles at the edges, for 8 to 12 hours. Turn off the heat and let the stock cool down, uncovered, for 1 hour.

3. Using tongs or a slotted spoon, carefully remove the bones from the stock and discard them. Line a fine sieve with several layers of cheesecloth. Using a ladle, carefully strain the stock through the sieve into a clean metal container.

4. Place the metal container in a cold ice water bath. Stir the liquid regularly as it cools down. As the stock cools, it may be necessary to add more ice. The entire batch must be cooled down to 40° F/4.4°C.

5. You may use the stock immediately or portion it into containers and store it, covered, in the refrigerator for up to 7 days or in the freezer for up to 6 months. Skim the fat from the surface and bring to a full boil before using.

Note: Don't worry about skimming the fat from the top of the stock as it simmers. The fat will keep the stock fresh by forming a seal in the refrigerator or freezer, and it is easily removed before you reheat the stock.

chicken stock

YIELD: 2 QUARTS (2 L)

4 POUNDS (1.8 KG) CHICKEN BONES AND PARTS (BACKS, NECKS, CARCASSES AND THIGHS)

3 QUARTS (3 L) COLD WATER

2 MEDIUM ONIONS, COARSELY CHOPPED

2 CARROTS, CUT INTO 1/2-INCH (1.25 CM) CHUNKS

2 STALKS CELERY, CUT INTO 1/2-INCH (1.25 CM) CHUNKS

2 MEDIUM TOMATOES, CUT INTO CHUNKS

1 LEEK, WHITE AND LIGHT GREEN PARTS ONLY, WASHED AND CUT INTO 1/2-INCH (1.25 CM) CHUNKS

3 SPRIGS PARSLEY, WITH STEMS

3 SPRIGS THYME

6 WHOLE BLACK PEPPERCORNS

1. Rinse the chicken bones and parts well under cold running water and place them in a stockpot. Add the cold water and slowly bring to a boil, uncovered, over medium-low heat. Reduce the heat to very low and simmer very gently, with just a few bubbles at the edges, for 4 hours. Use a slotted spoon or ladle to skim the froth and foam from the surface occasionally.

2. Add the remaining ingredients to the stock and simmer for 1 hour more. Turn off the heat and let the stock cool down, uncovered, for 30 minutes.

3. Using tongs or a slotted spoon, carefully remove the bones from the stock and discard them. Strain the stock through a fine sieve into a clean metal container and discard the vegetables left behind. For a very clear stock, strain the stock again, this time through a fine sieve lined with several layers of cheesecloth.

4. Place the metal container in a cold ice water bath. Stir the liquid regularly as it cools down. As the stock cools, it may be necessary to drain out some of the warm water and replace it with some ice. The entire batch must be cooled down to 40° F/4.4°C.

5. You may use the stock immediately or portion it into containers and store it, covered, in the refrigerator for up to 7 days or in the freezer for up to 6 months. Skim the fat from the surface and bring to a full boil before using.

Note: To make a darker stock suitable for use in making brown sauces, roast the chicken bones first, as described in the recipe for beef stock, before adding the cold water.

vegetable stock

2 TABLESPOONS VEGETABLE OIL

1 WHITE ONION, SLICED

1 LEEK, GREEN AND WHITE
PARTS, CHOPPED

2 STALKS CELERY, CHOPPED

1 CUP (140 G) GREEN CABBAGE,
CHOPPED

2 CARROTS, PEELED, TRIMMED
AND CHOPPED

1 TURNIP, PEELED,
TRIMMED AND CHOPPED

2 TOMATOES, SEEDED AND
CHOPPED

1 1/2 CLOVES GARLIC, CRUSHED

2 1/4 QUARTS (2.25 L) WATER,
COLD

3 SPRIGS PARSLEY, CLEANED
WITH STEMS

3 SPRIGS THYME

6 WHOLE BLACK PEPPERCORNS

1. Heat the oil in a stock pot.

2. Add the onions, leeks, celery, turnips, carrots, cabbage and tomatoes to the stick pot. Sweat the vegetables for 8 to 10 minutes until they soften and become translucent. Make sure they do not brown.

3. Add the water and the remaining ingredients. Bring the water to a simmer and let it cook uncovered for 30 to 40 minutes.

4. Strain the stock through a fine sieve into a clean metal container and discard the vegetables left behind. For a very clear stock, strain the stock again, this time through a fine sieve lined with several layers of cheesecloth.

5. Place the metal container in a cold water bath. Stir the liquid regularly as it cools down. As the stock cools, it may be necessary to replace the warm water with some new ice. The entire batch must be cooled down to 40° F/4.4°C.

6. You may use the stock immediately or portion it into containers and store it, covered, in the refrigerator for up to 7 days or in the freezer for up to 6 months. Skim the fat from the surface and bring to a full boil before using.

fish stock

3 POUNDS (1.3 KG) FISH BONES AND CARCASSES (SEE NOTE, BELOW)

2 FISH HEADS, GILLS REMOVED

2 TABLESPOONS UNSALTED BUTTER

2 LARGE ONIONS, THINLY SLICED

5 MEDIUM STALKS CELERY, THINLY SLICED

2 CARROTS, THINLY SLICED

1/4 CUP (35 G) COARSELY CHOPPED FRESH PARSLEY LEAVES AND STEMS

2 BAY SMALL LEAVES

10 SPRIGS THYME

2 TABLESPOONS WHOLE BLACK PEPPERCORNS

1/4 CUP (60 ML) DRY WHITE WINE

6 CUPS (1.5 L) HOT WATER, PLUS EXTRA AS NEEDED

1. With a heavy knife or kitchen scissors, cut the fish bones into approximate 6-inch (15 cm) pieces. Rinse the fish bones and heads well under cold running water and set aside.

2. In a large stockpot, heat the butter over low heat. Add the onions, celery, carrots, parsley, bay leaves, thyme and peppercorns. Cook, stirring frequently, until the vegetables soften and become translucent, about 8 to 10 minutes (do not let the vegetables brown).

3. Add the wine to the vegetables and place the fish bones and heads on top. Add enough hot water to barely cover the ingredients and stir gently to mix. Increase the heat to medium and bring to a simmer. Reduce the heat to low and simmer very gently, with just a few bubbles at the edges, for 20 minutes. Turn off the heat, cover the pan and let the stock sit for 10 minutes.

4. Place the metal container in a cold water bath. Stir the liquid regularly as it cools down. As the stock cools, it may be necessary to replace the warm water with some fresh ice. The entire batch must be cooled down to 40°F/4.4°C.

5. Strain the stock through a fine sieve into a clean pot and discard the solids left behind. For a very clear stock, strain the stock again, this time through a fine sieve lined with several layers of cheesecloth. You may use the stock immediately or portion it into containers and store it, covered, in the refrigerator for up to 7 days or in the freezer for up to 6 months.

Note: Ask your fishmonger to save bones and/or heads for you. A fishmonger is the person in the market who properly handles, ices and transports the fish. He or she should be able to answer questions regarding the fish's origin and its qualities. Any mild to moderate fish will do, including rockfish, snapper, cod and flounder.

Variations:

SHRIMP STOCK: Stir shrimp shells into the cooked vegetables at the end of Step 2. Sauté until the shells turn pink, then add the wine and fish bones and make the stock as directed. (Use shrimp shells you've saved and frozen from other recipes that require shrimp to be cooked out of the shell.)

SEAFOOD STOCK: Chop crab, lobster or crayfish shells and cook them with the vegetables before adding the wine and fish bones.

CLAM ENRICHED STOCK: Steam a few pounds of clams in 1 cup (250 ml) dry white wine or water (for the technique, see Linguine Del Giorno, page 60). After steaming, strain the liquid well through several layers of wet cheesecloth and add it to the fish stock. Use the clam meat for chowder, clam dip or other recipes.

cook's notes:
a glossary of cooking terms

Al dente "To the tooth"; to cook an item, such as pasta or vegetables, until it is tender, but still firm.

Au jus Served with its natural juices, which are usually unthickened pan drippings.

Baste To moisten food during cooking with pan drippings, sauce or other liquid. Basting prevents food from drying out.

Barbecue To cook on a grill or spit over hot coals, or in an enclosed pit, often with a seasoned marinade or basting sauce. A roasting or grilling technique.

Blanch To cook an item partially and very briefly in boiling water or in hot fat. Usually it is a preparation technique, to loosen peels from vegetables, fruits and nuts.

Boil To cook in water or other liquid that is bubbling rapidly, at about 212°F/100°C.

Bouquet garni A mixture of herbs and spices tied in a cheesecloth bag.

Braise To cook items such as meat, covered, in a small amount of liquid, usually after browning them first. To cook certain vegetables slowly in a small amount of liquid without the preliminary browning.

Broil To cook with radiant heat from above.

Caramelization The browning of sugars caused by heat.

Carry-over cooking The rise in temperature in the inside of roasted meat after it is removed from the oven.

Chef's knife An all-purpose knife used for chopping, slicing and mincing. Its blade is usually between 8 and 14 inches long (20-35 cm).

Clarified butter Purified butterfat, with water and milk solids removed.

Concassé To chop coarsely.

Deglaze To use a liquid, such as wine, water or stock, to dissolve food particles and/or caramelized drippings left in a pan after roasting or sautéing.

Degrease To skim the fat off of the surface of a liquid, such as a stock or sauce.

Dice To cut ingredients into small cubes.

Dredge To coat foods with a dry ingredient such as flour or bread crumbs.

Emulsion A mixture of two or more liquids, one of which is fat or oil and the other of

which is water-based, so that tiny globules of one are suspended in the other. This may involve the use of stabilizers, such as egg or mustard.

Fillet, Filet A boneless cut of meat, fish, or poultry.

French knife See Chef's knife.

Fricassée A stew of poultry or other white meat, with a white sauce.

Fry To cook in hot fat.

Griddle A flat, solid cooking surface.

Grill A cooking technique in which foods are cooked by a radiant heat source placed below the food. Also, a piece of equipment on which grilling is done.

Julienne To cut into thin strips.

Jus Unthickened juices from a roast.

Liaison A mixture of cream and eggs used to thicken sauces.

Marinate To soak food in a seasoned liquid.

Mince To chop into very fine pieces.

Mirepoix A combination of chopped, aromatic vegetables— usually two parts onion, one part carrot, one part celery— used to flavor stocks, soups, braises and stews.

Mise en place "Put in place." The preparation and assembly of ingredients, pans, and utensils needed for a certain dish.

Pan-broil To cook uncovered in a sauté pan or skillet without fat.

Pan-fry To cook in a moderate amount of fat in an uncovered pan.

Pan gravy A sauce made by deglazing pan drippings from a roast and combining them with a roux or other starch and additional stock.

Parboil To cook partially in a boiling or simmering liquid.

Parcook To partially cook an item before storing or finishing by another method.

Poach A method in which items are cooked gently in simmering liquid.

Puff pastry A very light, flaky pastry made from a dough that's rolled and folded several times creating hundreds of layers that puff up from baking.

Purée A food product that has been mashed or strained to a smooth pulp, or the process of making such a product.

Reduce To cook by simmering or boiling until the quantity is decreased; often done to concentrate flavors.

Reduction The product that results when a liquid is reduced.

Roast To cook foods by surrounding them with hot, dry air, in an oven or a spit over an open fire.

Roux A cooked mixture of equal parts flour and fat.

Sauté To quickly cook in a small amount of fat.

Scald To heat a liquid, usually milk or cream, to just below the boiling point.

Score To cut the surface of an item at regular intervals to allow it to cook regularly.

Sear To brown the surface of a food quickly at high temperatures.

Simmer To maintain the temperature of a liquid just below the boiling point.

Steaming A cooking method by which items are cooked in a vapor bath created by boiling water or other liquids.

Stir-fry A cooking method similar to sautéing in which the items are cooked over very high heat, using little fat, and the food is kept moving constantly.

Sweat To cook an item, usually vegetables, in a covered pan with a small amount of fat until they are softened and release moisture.

Temper To raise the temperature of a cold liquid gradually by slowly stirring in a hot liquid.

Truss To tie up meat or poultry with a string before cooking in order to give it a more compact shape for more even cooking and better appearance.

Vent To allow the circulation or escape of a liquid or gas.

Zest The colored part of the peel of citrus fruits.

conversion scales

WEIGHTS

$1/2$ ounce	=	14 grams
$3/4$ ounce	=	21 grams
1 ounce	=	28 grams
$1^{1/4}$ ounces	=	35 grams
$1^{1/2}$ ounces	=	43 grams
$1^{3/4}$ ounces	=	50 grams
2 ounces	=	57 grams
$2^{1/4}$ ounces	=	64 grams
$2^{1/2}$ ounces	=	71 grams
$2^{3/4}$ ounces	=	78 grams
3 ounces	=	85 grams
$3^{1/4}$ ounces	=	92 grams
$3^{1/2}$ ounces	=	99 grams
4 ounces	=	114 grams
5 ounces	=	142 grams
6 ounces	=	170 grams
7 ounces	=	199 grams
8 ounces	=	226 grams
9 ounces	=	254 grams
10 ounces	=	283 grams
11 ounces	=	311 grams
12 ounces	=	340 grams
13 ounces	=	368 grams
14 ounces	=	396 grams
15 ounces	=	425 grams
1 pound	=	453 grams
$1^{1/4}$ pounds	=	566 grams
$1^{1/2}$ pounds	=	679 grams
$1^{3/4}$ pounds	=	792 grams
2 pounds	=	905 grams
$2^{1/4}$ pounds	=	1,018 grams
$2^{1/2}$ pounds	=	1,133 grams
$2^{3/4}$ pounds	=	1,246 grams

LIQUID MEASURES

1 teaspoon	=	0.005 liter	$1^{1/2}$ cups	=	0.36 liter
1 tablespoon	=	0.015 liter	$1^{3/4}$ cups	=	0.42 liter
2 tablespoons	=	0.03 liter	1 pint	=	0.47 liter
$1/4$ cup	=	0.06 liter	$1^{1/4}$ pints	=	0.60 liter
$1/2$ cup	=	0.12 liter	$1^{1/2}$ pints	=	0.72 liter
1 cup	=	0.18 liter	$1^{3/4}$ pints	=	0.83 liter
$1^{1/4}$ cups	=	0.30 liter	1 quart	=	0.94 liter

U.S. WEIGHTS AND MEASURES

1 pinch = less than $1/8$ teaspoon (dry)

1 dash = 3 drops to $1/4$ teaspoon (liquid)

3 teaspoons = 1 tablespoon = $1/2$ ounce (liquid and dry)

4 tablespoons = 2 ounces (liquid and dry) = $1/4$ cup

$5^{1/3}$ tablespoons = $1/3$ cup

16 tablespoons = 8 ounces = 1 cup = $1/2$ pound

16 tablespoons = 48 teaspoons

32 tablespoons = 16 ounces = 2 cups = 1 pound

64 tablespoons = 32 ounces = 1 quart = 2 pounds

1 cup = 8 ounces (liquid) = $1/2$ pint

2 cups = 16 ounces (liquid) = 1 pint

4 cups = 32 ounces (liquid) = 2 pints = 1 quart

16 cups = 128 ounces (liquid) = 4 quarts = 1 gallon

1 quart = 2 pints (dry)

8 quarts = 1 peck (dry)

4 pecks = 1 bushel (dry)

APPROXIMATE EQUIVALENTS

1 quart (liquid) = about 1 liter

8 tablespoons = 4 ounces = $1/2$ cup = 1 stick butter

1 cup all-purpose presifted flour = 5 ounces

1 cup stoneground yellow cornmeal = $4^{1/2}$ ounces

1 cup granulated sugar = 8 ounces

1 cup brown sugar = 6 ounces

1 cup confectioners' sugar = $4^{1/2}$ ounces

1 large egg = 2 ounces = $1/4$ cup = 4 tablespoons

1 egg yolk = 1 tablespoon + 1 teaspoon

1 egg white = 2 tablespoons + 2 teaspoons

index

ROYAL CULINARY COLLECTIONS™